[

HIGHLIGHTS OF THE
OLYMPICS

THE IMPORTANT THING IN
THE OLYMPIC GAMES IS NOT
WINNING BUT TAKING PART.
THE ESSENTIAL THING IN
LIFE IS NOT CONQUERING
BUT FIGHTING WELL.

BARON de COUBERTIN

HIGHLIGHTS
OF THE
OLYMPICS

FROM ANCIENT TIMES TO THE PRESENT

By JOHN DURANT

HASTINGS HOUSE PUBLISHERS · NEW YORK 22

METRIC DISTANCES CONVERSION TABLE

Meters	Miles	Yards	Feet	Inches
100	0	109	1	1
400	0	437	1	4⅜
800	0	874	2	8¾
1500	0	1640	1	4¾
3000	1	1520	2	8¾
5000	3	188	0	8½
10000	6	376	1	2¼

The Marathon is 42 kilometers, 195 meters in length, which is the equivalent of 26 miles, 385 yards.

Published simultaneously in Canada
by S. J. Reginald Saunders, Publishers, Toronto 2B.

Library of Congress Catalog Card Number: 60-14616
Printed in the United States of America

CONTENTS

INTRODUCTION

There are 21 sports recognized by the International Olympic Committee and of these the oldest and largest (in number of competitors) is track and field, sometimes called "athletics." More athletes and more nations take part in it than in any other Olympic sport, and it attracts the greatest crowds and creates the most interest throughout the world. Indeed, it is the heart of the Olympic Games and has been ever since they began in ancient Greece. Even the Olympic motto, *"Citius, Altius, Fortius"* is directed to the track and field athlete, for the Latin words mean "Swifter, Higher, Stronger," to encourage him to run faster, jump higher, and throw more strongly.

CHAPTER **1**

THE ANCIENT GAMES

ONE SUMMER AFTERNOON in 776 B.C. a crowd of some 45,000 Greeks seated on the grassy slopes of the stadium at Olympia rose up and cheered as a naked runner burst out ahead of his rivals on the straightaway track and led them across the finish line. The winner was Coroebus, a cook from the nearby city of Elis. It was a dash to glory for Coroebus, for by winning the race of approximately 200 yards he became the first victor of record of the Olympic Games.

The Games had probably been in existence several years before Coroebus sprinted into history but because no records were kept until his time the year 776 B.C. is considered to be the date of the First Olympiad. Indeed, it is the first definite date of any event in all Greek history. From that year on the Olympic Games were held every four years for nearly 1,200 years without a single interruption.

Nothing was more important to the Greeks. They would not allow anything to interfere with them, not even wars. In 480 B.C., on the very day the battle of Thermopylae was fought between the Greeks and the invading Persians — in fact, the fate of the nation was hanging in the balance — the usual thousands of sports fans sat in the stadium at Olympia and watched the finals of the boxing tournament.

Nowadays the Olympics are called off when war breaks out, but it was just the opposite in ancient times. The various city-states that made up the Greek nation were constantly at war with one another, but during the month of the Olympic festival a truce was proclaimed

7

and all trading between cities was suspended. In this way the whole country could take time off to pay tribute to its manhood at Olympia.

Because ancient war was largely man-to-man combat, it was essential for the young men of Greece to keep in good condition at all times, for they might be called upon to defend their soil at a moment's notice. The development of physical strength and skill was the real purpose of the many athletic contests held throughout Greece, the oldest and largest of which was the Olympic Games.

"There is no greater glory for a man as long as he lives than that which he wins by his own hands and feet," Homer said in the *Odyssey,* the great epic poem of Greece.

No heroes were ever glorified as were the Olympic champions, not even victorious generals returning from war. From the moment an athlete was crowned with a wreath of wild olive, which was the symbol of victory, his name was proclaimed throughout the nation. Odes were written in his honor by the greatest poets of the age and were sung by choirs of youths. His deeds were chiseled on stone pillars and sculptors shaped his likeness in life-size statutes. A whole city would turn out to welcome home a victorious son and escort him in triumph through the streets.

When Exaenetus, winner of a foot race, returned to his native city, Agrigentum, he was drawn in a four-horse chariot and was escorted by 300 of the chief citizens, each riding in a chariot pulled by a pair of white horses.

Sometimes the citizens would honor their hero by knocking down a section of the city's walls so that he could drive through the opening instead of the gate. This symbolic gesture meant that with such a famous champion living in the city there was no longer any need for walls for protection against the enemy. In addition to such honors, an Olympic victor was often exempted from taxation for life and given expensive presents, and even sums of money, depending upon the wealth of the honored city.

The Greeks chose the loveliest spot in the land to celebrate the Games. The site was the sacred valley of Olympia, a broad, fertile plain on the western coast of the Grecian peninsula which juts out into the blue waters of the Mediterranean Sea. Surrounding the pleasant valley were high mountains and groves of pine and olive trees, and through it ran the winding river, Alpheus.

8

Above, Olympic runners in a long-distance race in 333 B.C. (from a Grecian Vase). Below, Greek athletes exercising in a gymnasium. The man on the left is carrying "halteres" or weights, to give him added distance in the broad jump. With him are two javelin throwers and a discus thrower (second from left).

From the dawn of history the ancients had assembled on these meadowlands to honor their gods, many of whom, they believed, lived on the heights of Mount Olympus. At first the gatherings were simple religious festivals and were observed only by those who lived in western Greece. Gradually the place attracted more and more worshipers, and games and contests were added to the festivals.

All kinds of structures began to spring up on the grounds — shrines, altars, temples, a museum, a gymnasium, baths, a stadium, and a hippodrome for chariot races. At length Olympia grew to be a permanent holy city and was looked upon as the capital of the Greek world. The Olympic Games became the greatest festival of the mighty nation that at one time extended into Africa and as far east as India. They were famous throughout the civilized world.

Only freeborn Greek citizens were allowed to compete in them. The athletes (from *athlos,* a contest) were selected after elimination trials held in various parts of the country. The outstanding performers of the trial meets came to Olympia, where for 10 months they submitted to a tough training grind under professional coaches and trainers. They lived in the gymnasium (from *gymnos,* naked) and practiced all day long, every day, with no time off for relaxation or pleasure of any kind. At the end of that period they were ready for the Olympic Games. The last thing they did before appearing on the field was to take an oath to observe all the rules and to maintain the ideals of sportsmanship.

In the beginning the contests were limited to foot races, the first of which was the *stade.* From this race we get our word "stadium." It was run on a sandy track the length of the athletic field inside the stadium. This was the 200-yard dash that was won by Coroebus, the flying cook.

Later a second race of two *stades* was added, in which the runners sprinted the length of the track, turned quickly and then raced back to the starting point. Still later an endurance race of 12 *stades* was put on the program. In 708 B.C. the pentathlon (described later) and wrestling were introduced. More and more events, including chariot races, were added as time went on.

Perhaps the greatest Olympic star was Milo of Croton, a physical marvel who flourished in the sixth century B.C. and won the wrestling crown at Olympia six times. He was never defeated. For generations the Greeks sang and wrote of his feats. He was said to have developed his fabulous strength by carrying a calf on his shoulders every day of its life until it was a full-grown bull.

Many were the tricks that Milo performed for his admirers. He would hold a pomegranate in his fist so firmly that no one could force open his fingers to touch it, yet so controlled was his grip that he never crushed or damaged the fruit. He would stand barefooted on an oiled and slippery discus and challenge anyone to push or rush him off it. No one could budge him.

Arrachion, though dead, is the winner of the pancratian as his opponent raises his right hand to the judges, thereby acknowledging defeat.

The pancratian was a combination of boxing and wrestling and was supervised by a referee (right) to see that the rules were not broken. This bout took place in 332 B.C.

Milo would tie a cord around his forehead, then take a deep breath and hold it until the veins in his head swelled up to a point where the cord burst. What a man was Milo!

No less a man was Polydamas of Thessaly, champion of the pancratian, which was a fierce combination of boxing and wrestling. Polydamas once killed a lion with his bare hands. At another time he stopped a chariot going at full speed simply by seizing the back of it with one hand.

Another pancratian champion of everlasting fame was Arrachion of Phigalia, who was awarded the crown of victory as he lay dead in the stadium. During the final match of the pancratian, an event in which no holds or punches of any kind were barred, Arrachion was being strangled by his opponent, but as he was losing consciousness he grabbed his rival's right foot and twisted it out of its socket. This caused his opponent such intense pain that he raised his hand to the referee, thereby acknowledging defeat. At that instant Arrachion gasped his last breath — yet he was the winner.

One of the most sought-after crowns was the five-event pentathlon, which was designed to determine the best all-around athlete. It was a severe test demanding skill, strength, courage, and endurance, and it was held in high esteem by the ancients. The philosopher, Aristotle, who was critical of the one-sided development of the specialized performer such as the boxer and the wrestler, had only praise for the beautifully proportioned athletes of the pentathlon. More than any others, these men achieved the Greek ideal of physical perfection.

According to some accounts, the pentathlon was an elimination tournament that began with all the contestants taking part in the broad jump. Those who jumped a certain distance — how far is not known — qualified for the next event, which was the javelin throw. The four men who threw the javelin the farthest then took part in the next test on the program, the one-*stade* race. Here, the athlete who ran last was eliminated, leaving three for the discus throw. The two who tossed the 12-pound discus the greatest distance then came to grips in the grand finale, a wrestling match to the finish.

In this final test the first man gaining three falls was declared the winner of the pentathlon. A fall, however, did not consist of pinning a man's shoulders to the ground, as it does today. In the so-called "upright wrestling" of the ancient Games a fall was counted when a man was thrown to the ground. If both wrestlers fell together, nothing was counted, and they started over. The ancient wrestler tried to toss his opponent cleanly to the ground and he often used an over-the-shoulder hold that is known in modern wrestling as the "flying mare."

The type of wrestling used in the pancratian, however, was "ground wrestling," in which the battle continued on the ground. In the rough-and-tumble pancratian, or game of all powers, the contestants began by facing each other standing upright and tried to get one another down by punching, wrestling, or even kicking. When a man went down, his opponent could jump on him, kick him anywhere, sit astride him and pummel him with his fists, strangle him or break his bones with any kind of a wrestling grip. Just about everything was allowed except biting and eye gouging. The battle went on to a finish, without any rest periods, and ended when a man lay unconscious or was so badly beaten that he held up his hand in sign of defeat.

Brutal as the pancratian was, it was a fair test that required more skill than strength, and certainly lots of courage. It was designed to prepare men for the death struggle in real warfare. Although the rules were few, they were strictly enforced by a referee who stood by with

The hoplite was a foot race in armor of two *stades* distance and it was introduced at Olympia in 520 B.C.

a stout rod. At the slightest violation of the rules he would give the offender a solid whack with the rod. This method of supervision, by the way, was used in all the Olympic events. The officials were well trained and honest, and always dealt fairly with the competitors.

In 520 B.C. the hoplite, a foot race in armor, was initiated at Olympia. The runners carried heavy round shields, and wore plumed helmets and nothing else. The distance was two *stades*.

This was the last important event added to the festival, except for various chariot races. The Games were now approaching their zenith, which was reached during the fifth and fourth centuries B.C. Then, when Greece began to decline as a world power and Rome rose to eminence, the Games showed the first signs of decay. Slowly they lost the amateur spirit and the religious atmosphere of the old days.

Aristophanes, the Athenian playwright, was well aware of the decline. Bitterly he complained that the young men of Greece had deserted the gymnasiums for the luxuries of the baths and were pale-faced and narrow-chested. It was true. The long months of rigorous training that had brought glory to their fathers no longer appealed to the youth of the land. The big cities began to hire professional athletes in their place. Many of them were foreigners and according to the rules were not eligible to compete. The Greeks simply nationalized them and made them eligible.

The low estate of the Games was evident in A.D. 67 when the egotistical Roman emperor, Nero, came to Olympia with a retinue of 5,000 people who were brought along to applaud him. Greece had long since been conquered by Rome and was now merely a province of the imperial city. Nero entered the chariot races and several competitions for singing and playing musical instruments. In the 10-horse chariot race he took a spill but the fawning officials picked him up, put him back in the chariot, and finally gave him first prize. In all the other competitions he also was awarded crowns, and he proclaimed the victories by making the announcements himself. Such was the decline of the once lofty Olympic Games.

The end was in sight. The last known victor was an Armenian prince named Varastades, who won the boxing crown in the 291st Olympiad, about A.D. 390. This date is not certain, for the records of the later Games have been lost. In A.D. 394 the Christian emperor of Rome, Theodosius I, abolished the Games on the ground that they were a pagan festival. Soon barbarian invaders pillaged the Olympic buildings and then, as if the gods were angered, earthquakes lowered those that remained. Later the Alpheus River changed its course and covered the hallowed ground with silt.

The end of the old Olympics was complete, but the modern world owes much to the ancient Greeks. They were the first to organize and make rules for games, and to bring sport to a high level. They developed the gymnasium and the first training methods and wrote the first code of sportsmanship. They set the standard for fair play. It is because of the Grecks that we have the Olympic Games today.

Baron Pierre de Coubertin, the French nobleman who brought the Olympic Games back to life.

CHAPTER 2

THE GAMES ARE REVIVED

ON THE AFTERNOON of April 6, 1896, a crowd of 50,000 seated in the stadium at Athens and perhaps as many more thousands watching from the surrounding hills, saw a small, wiry youth mount the winner's stand on the field and receive the olive wreath of victory on his brow. As he stood there the band struck up "The Star Spangled Banner," the American flag was raised to the top of a 200-foot pole, and a group of Yankee sailors on shore leave from the U.S.S. *San Francisco* roared their approval.

The honored youth was a Harvard student named James B. Connolly, victor in the "triple jump" or hop, step, and jump, which was the first final event on the Olympic program. Connolly thus became the first Olympic champion since Varastades won the boxing title some 1,500 years before.

Seated in the royal box alongside the King and Queen of Greece and undoubtedly more thrilled than Connolly himself was Baron Pierre de Coubertin, a tireless little Frenchman who for years had staged a one-man campaign to bring the Olympic Games back to life. He was seeing his dreams come true at last.

Baron de Coubertin, the founder of the modern Games, was born in Paris on January 1, 1863. He was educated at St. Cyr, the famous French military academy, but army life did not appeal to him and he resigned his commission. Still vivid and painful to most Frenchmen at that time were the memories of the Franco-Prussian War of 1870, in which France was defeated and overrun by Germans. The young men

17

of France had won no glory in that war. What was the reason? Was it that they lacked vigor, perhaps because competitive athletics and sports had no place in the French schools and universities? The situation was different in England and America, the young baron observed on his many visits to those countries. In the English-speaking nations athletics were an important part of the educational system. It was an established belief that competition on the field developed high qualities of character by encouraging clean living, sportsmanship, mental and physical agility, and courage.

Not so in France, where games were thought to interfere with study and therefore students should not take part in them. The baron was convinced that this attitude toward sport was wrong and he decided to do something about it. Soon he was convinced that he should devote his life and modest fortune to the task of improving the youth of France through competitive sports and thus strengthen the manhood of the nation.

In the 1880's a group of German archaeologists had spent six years at Olympia digging up the buried city from the dust of ages. Their findings and restorations aroused great interest in the ancient Olympic Games throughout the world. The Germans, to their everlasting credit, did not remove a single piece of marble from the site. Many visitors were attracted to the place, and among them was Baron de Coubertin, who wandered about the ruined city and was greatly impressed by what he saw.

Perhaps it was there at Olympia, on the very field where Coroebus had raced to fame and Milo had downed his challengers, that Coubertin began to think of athletics not only for his beloved France but for the whole world. If there could be a universal understanding of amateurism, he reasoned, the athletes of all nations might compete on an equal basis and a great good would be accomplished. Why would it not be possible to revive the Olympic Games, he wondered. The thought gripped him more firmly every day.

In 1892, at a meeting at the Athletic Sports Union in Paris, Baron de Coubertin first publicly announced the Olympic Games idea. "Let us export oarsmen, runners, fencers," he said at the conference. "There is the free trade of the future — and on the day when it shall take place . . . the cause of peace will have received a new and powerful support."

The crowd at Athens in 1896 hails the revival of the ancient Olympic Games.

His listeners were cool to the proposal, but the baron refused to be discouraged. Although he was too small to be an athlete — he stood about 5 feet, 3 inches — he had the bulldog tenacity of the born competitor. For two years he worked tirelessly to stir up popular interest in his project. In 1894, at an international athletic congress attended by representatives of many nations, Coubertin again proposed that the Games be revived. This time it was a different story. The enthusiasm created by the little Frenchman spread among the delegates of the congress and they not only approved his idea, but set the time and place for the first modern Olympic Games. They voted unanimously to hold the Games in Athens, the capital of Greece, in April, 1896. They would have preferred to have the Games go to Olympia itself, but the ancient stadium there was beyond reconstruction.

For that matter, there was no stadium at Athens, either, and the Greek Government could not supply the funds to build one. Fortunately, a wealthy Greek merchant came to the rescue and paid the entire cost — about $386,000 — of restoring the Stadium of Herodis at Athens, which was originally built in 330 B.C.

Bob Garrett, captain of the Princeton track team, who won two gold medals for the United States at Athens in 1896.

In America there was very little publicity given to the announcement of the 1896 revival. There was no United States Olympic Committee, no Olympic team, and no money for the long trip to Greece. However, the idea of competing against other countries excited a small group of American track and field athletes, who decided to take part in the Games.

One was Robert S. Garrett, captain of the Princeton track team, who persuaded three college mates to go along with him, and paid all their expenses. Another was James B. Connolly, who was refused a leave of absence from Harvard University, but went anyway at his own expense, and never returned to graduate. Meanwhile, the Boston Athletic Association raised enough money to send five athletes, and that completed the unofficial 10-man American track and field team.

It was by no means a representative team. The only national champion on it was Tom Burke, a quarter-miler from Boston. The New York Athletic Club, which boasted several champions, was not interested enough to send a single man.

Despite their country's lack of support, the American athletes were spirited and determined, and they piled up a most remarkable record against 12 competing nations at Athens. There were 12 track and field events on the program. The Americans put men in every event except the 800-meter run and scored nine victories in 11 tries!

There were other contests besides track and field — shooting, fencing, swimming, tennis, cycling, wrestling, gymnastics, and weight lifting. America entered only the two shooting matches and won two first prizes. The main interest, however, was in track and field. This had been true since the Olympic Games of antiquity, and remains so today.

The Games were well attended, and the crowds were enthusiastic, even though the performances were on the mediocre side. The purpose of the Games, as Baron de Coubertin pointed out, was not to break records but to give the youth of the world a chance to meet and know one another on the friendly field of combat.

"The important thing in the Olympic Games is not winning but taking part. The essential thing in life is not conquering but fighting well." This is the Olympic Creed, stated by Coubertin himself, and the first modern Games lived up to that standard.

It was not all smooth sailing from then on, however. There were many wrinkles to be ironed out before the Games graduated from the experimental stage to achieve world-wide recognition. Not until 1912 did this happen. Meanwhile, the Games went through a rather painful growing-up stage. Let us take a brief look at those early Olympics.

The second Games were awarded to Paris in 1900, but the French were completely indifferent to the honor of holding them. They considered the Olympics merely a side attraction to the big Paris Exposition, an international fair that was taking place at the same time.

The 55 American athletes were stunned when they got their first look at the field on which the Games were to be held. There was no cinder track; there were no pits for the jumpers; the surface of the grassy field was uneven; there was not enough room for the discus and hammer throwers. Their shots landed in the trees alongside the small field. Most high schools in the United States had better athletic fields than this one.

The bored French officials marked off the various racing distances on the grass. The jumpers dug their own pits with their spiked shoes. Admission was free but the Games received so little publicity that less than 1,000 people bothered to look at them during the entire five days of the meet. There were more participants than spectators. Many Americans who had come to Paris to see the Exposition did not know that the Olympics were taking place right on the same grounds.

In spite of everything, new records were made in every event on the track and field program, and again the Americans stood out above the other 19 competing nations. They won 17 of the 23 events.

Four years later, in St. Louis, where the third Olympics were held, another world's fair was in progress, and again the Games played a minor role to a bigger event. European representation was so small that it did not amount to anything. England did not send a single man, nor did France, nor Sweden. The reason given was that St. Louis was so far away that it would cost too much to send teams there. Consequently, the Games were almost wholly an American affair. In some events there was not one foreign competitor. Small wonder, then, that the United States made such a good showing. In the 22 track and field events the Americans won 21 first-place gold medals. The sole foreign champion was Canada's Etienne Desmarteau, a Montreal policeman, who won the 56-pound weight throw.

Baron de Coubertin was disappointed in the way the Olympics were turning out. They had gotten off to a splendid start at Athens but since then they had gone downhill, not in number of contests and participants — indeed, the Games were getting larger in every way — but the true spirit of the Olympics was fading away. Instead of inspiring youth and promoting international good will, they were becoming a side show.

Hoping that a return to Athens would save them, Coubertin proposed that they be held there permanently every four years in addition to the regular Olympics. He suggested starting this new cycle in 1906, two years after the St. Louis Games and two years before the next ones, already scheduled for London in 1908. His plan was received with enthusiasm everywhere, especially in Greece, where the people went all out to make the Games a success.

Up to this time America's athletes had been sent to the Olympics by the various clubs and colleges they represented. They traveled independently and trained on their own. On the field they wore their club or college track suits with a small American flag pinned to the chest. At Athens for the first time the United States had an official Olympic team of 35 men. It was financed by public contributions and went abroad and trained as a unit. Proudly the men wore the United States Olympic uniform — a white shirt with the American shield sewed on the front, and white trunks with red, white, and blue stripes down the sides.

As in 1896, the huge stadium was filled to overflowing every day and many more thousands looked down upon the field from the hills. Attendance records were shattered. King George and Queen Olga and the entire royal family of Greece attended the contests each day. The king personally awarded medals to the winners and crowned them with olive wreaths from the sacred groves of Olympia. The wearers of the Stars and Stripes once more dominated the track and field contests with 11 victories out of 19 events. However, the Games surpassed all previous contests — in number of nations and athletes participating, and in splendor and enthusiasm. It was a step forward toward the Olympic ideal.

Unfortunately, however, the new plan did not survive. Four years later political unrest in Greece caused Olympic officials to cancel the Games and they were never revived there. Because the 1906 Olympics were held in an off year and were not continued, they are not today recognized as official by the International Olympic Committee, although they once were. The I.O.C. considers them the "Unofficial Olympic Games" and does not list them in its record books. To almost everyone else, though, they are official, just as much as any other Olympic Games — and that includes sports writers and historians, the man in the street, and most certainly those old-time athletes who received Olympic medals in the Athens stadium.

Returning to the original four-year cycle, the Olympics were held in 1908 in London and were bigger — though not better — than ever. The British deserve credit for organizing and running the Games efficiently, but the contests were marred by constant squabbles between English and American officials. Of the many clashes — and there was at least one every day — the most bitter resulted from the ruling of British officials in the running of the 400-meter final.

In this race were three runners from the United States and one Englishman, Wyndham Halswelle. The crowd, perhaps influenced by a British press which had been critical of the Yankees all during the Games, was expecting trouble — and it came. As the four men turned into the homestretch Halswelle was running third, behind W. C. Robbins of Harvard, who was leading, and J. C. Carpenter of Cornell. As Carpenter and Halswelle swung to the outside to pass Robbins, someone alongside the track shouted "Foul!" and a British official rushed out and broke the tape at the finish. A second later Carpenter crossed the line well in front, with Robbins second and the English runner third. The British then pronounced it "no race" and ordered it rerun on the last day of the meet. Furious American officials shouted that they had been robbed and refused to let the Yankee athletes rerun the race. So on the final day Wyndham Halswelle ran the course all by himself and won a gold medal.

In spite of the many mix-ups and unpleasant incidents, some of which were due to pompous British officialdom, there was general good will among the contestants and on that basis the Games were a success. The United States took 15 first places against Great Britain's eight in the 27-event track and field program.

Four years later, in 1912, on the eve of World War I, the Games went to Stockholm, and the Swedes staged the best of the Olympic series up to that time. The whole affair was perfectly conducted and the athletes were treated fairly and entertained royally. All of the 25 invading nations — which included such far-off countries as Japan, Chile, and Australia — went away glowing with friendly feelings toward the Swedes. It was at this time that the Olympics, after faltering now and then on their way, seemed to reach maturity. At this time also the Games produced their first great individual star in the person of Jim Thorpe, the American Indian.

Jim Thorpe, the great Indian, as a track star.

Above, A Greek Olympic discus thrower in the backward swing, about 500 B.C. *Left,* Alvin C. Kraenzlein, the first Olympic athlete to win four gold medals in one set of Games (in Paris, 1900).

CHAPTER 3

BRIGHT PATH,
THE ALL-TIME GREATEST

BEFORE DESCRIBING THE DEEDS of the incomparable Thorpe, however, brief mention should be made of a few of the performers who stood out in the Olympics previous to his arrival.

The name of Bob Garrett is first on the list. When the stocky Princetonian decided to go to Athens in 1896 and try some of the field events, he heard that the ancient sport of hurling the discus was going to be on the program. The event was unknown in the United States and Bob had never seen a discus. He had a Princeton classmate make him one of steel and Bob practiced with the crude imitation for a couple of weeks before setting sail for Athens.

The Greeks had originated the discus throw and for centuries had excelled in it. They were sure that their unbeaten champion Parakevopoulos could not be vanquished. Cheers resounded in the stadium at Athens when he made his opening toss. Then Bob Garrett picked up the discus and made a startling discovery. It was much lighter and easier to handle than the homemade one he had practiced with in New Jersey! Bob whirled and heaved and sent it winging far beyond the Greek champion's best mark.

After winning this event, Bob tried the 16-pound shot and brought another victory to America. As if this wasn't enough, he entered the broad jump and high jump and got second place in each event. Bob was the headliner of the 1896 Games.

At Paris four years later a lanky 19-year-old flash from the University of Pennsylvania named Alvin C. Kraenzlein performed the astonishing feat of winning four individual championships. This all-around marvel broke the tape in the 60-meter sprint, the 110-meter high hurdles, the 200-meter low hurdles, and then stepped up and won the running broad jump. More than that, he made new records in all four events.

Only two other men have won four gold medals in one Olympic in the entire history of the Games — Paavo Nurmi and Jesse Owens, of whom we shall hear more in this book. Superb though these men were, they did not quite equal Kraenzlein's record, as only three of their four victories counted as individual championships. Nurmi and Owens won their fourth gold medals in team and relay races.

Kraenzlein's feat, then, stands alone, and it will never be equaled because contestants are now limited to three individual events in the Olympics. The Pennsylvania wonder was way ahead of his time in athletic ability. He made several intercollegiate, national, Olympic, and world records, and many of them stood for years. So famous was he in his day that the Germans engaged him to come to their country and build up an Olympic track and field team there.

Another man who was in a class by himself in those days was Ray C. Ewry, who went to his first Olympic Games in Paris in 1900 at the late track age of 27.

Ray had been a frail boy, an invalid half the time, and the family doctor advised him to take exercise to build up his body. Ray tried track and began to specialize in the jumps. In time he developed a pair of legs that seemed to be made of steel springs. No one could beat him in the three standing jumps — the high jump, broad jump, and hop, step, and jump.

The standing jumps are no longer on the Olympic slate but while they were — from 1900 to 1912 — they attracted a great deal of competition and, of course, counted just as much as any of the other events.

Ray Ewry, the long-legged fellow from Purdue, won so often that it became monotonous. In the 1900 Games he won all three standing jumps and in 1904 he again won all three. In Athens two years later, at the so-called Unofficial Games, Ray won two more gold medals. Why not three, as before? Because the standing hop, step, and jump was no longer on the program and Ray could compete in only two events! So it was when he went to London in 1908 and won the standing broad jump and the standing high jump. He was then 35 years old and decided to retire, perhaps so that he would have time to count his Olympic gold medals. He won 10 in all, three more than any other athlete has ever won in the Olympics.

Now we come to Jim Thorpe, the shining star of the 1912 Games at Stockholm. The tribal name of this great Sac and Fox Indian was Bright Path, and his path to athletic glory was indeed bright, although spotted by some dark shadows.

The black-haired Indian lad, Bright Path, was brought up on a ranch in Oklahoma and from the very start had the speed of a deer in his legs. His best sport was riding wild ponies. "I never saw one on the ranches that I could not catch, saddle, and ride," he recalled in later years.

Jim's dazzling speed and love of all sports made him a standout on the playing fields of the Carlisle Indian School in Pennsylvania, where he went at the age of 15 to learn to be a tailor. Carlisle was

America's Ray Ewry, a specialist in the standing jumps, won a total of 10 gold medals, more than any other Olympic athlete.

Jim Thorpe, the All-American football player

more of a vocational school than a college and numbered less than 1,000 Indians, half of them girls. Even so, the little school played football against large colleges and universities and more than held its own with them.

Jim was a substitute halfback in 1907 when he was but 18 and had only 155 pounds spread over his rangy six feet. That season the Indians beat such football powers as Minnesota, Penn, Syracuse, Harvard, and Penn State, losing only to Princeton.

Bright Path was still raw and knew nothing about faking when he ran with the ball, yet he often broke away like one of the wild ponies he used to chase and would go through a whole team for 80 yards or more. He was an amazingly talented kicker. He could punt more than 70 yards and kick field goals up to 50 yards from any angle. He could pass beautifully, and as a tackler he was deadly.

Next year he came back to the school 15 pounds heavier and was a regular on the varsity. The football team he played on beat Penn, Syracuse, Navy, Pitt, and Nebraska. That spring Jim tried baseball and track and immediately became Carlisle's finest in both sports. He was a slugging first baseman and in track was unbeatable as a hurdler, sprinter, and high jumper.

There was no question that Bright Path, the boy who could do everything, was an athletic genius. Unfortunately, he was inclined to be lazy and did not like to train. Easy-going Jim could never get mad no matter how hard the game was and he never exerted himself any more than he had to.

When Carlisle closed in the spring of 1909, Jim agreed to play semi-professional baseball in an obscure league in North Carolina. He thought nothing of accepting a little expense money, for this was a common practice then among college boys. The amateur rules in those days were not so strictly enforced as they are now. Jim had no idea that he might be endangering his amateur standing by taking money for playing a game he loved. He made no secret about it and used his own proud name, James C. Thorpe.

Jim went back to Oklahoma after playing summer ball and worked on a ranch instead of returning to Carlisle. He stayed out of school for two years, until at the urging of the Carlisle coach he decided to come back. Jim was itching to carry a football again. He was then 22 years old, weighed around 185 pounds, and had gained a lot of strength working on the ranch. He was still panther-fast.

That fall he was a sensation on the gridiron. Against Harvard, the champion of college football and undefeated in 1910, Jim tore the crimson line to shreds and kicked four field goals to win the game virtually single-handed, 18 to 15. The big Indian was superb in every game and at the end of the season won a place on Walter Camp's All-American first team.

Percy Haughton, the scholarly Harvard coach, said of Thorpe: "Watching him run the ends, slash off tackle, kick and pass and tackle, I realized that here was the theoretical super-player in flesh and blood."

The following spring Jim became known in college circles as Carlisle's one-man track team, perhaps because of his performance against Lafayette College at Easton, Pennsylvania, on May 25, 1912.

When Glenn (Pop) Warner, Carlisle's football and track coach, got off the train at Easton, the Lafayette officials who met him at the station were dismayed to find that only seven Indians were with him.

"Where is your track team?" he was asked.

"This is it," replied Pop, pointing to the seven Braves.

"But it will be no contest," said the Lafayette coach, Dr. Harold A. Bruce. "We have 48 men against you and we are undefeated this year."

"That's fine," smiled Pop, "but you'd better not make a bet on your boys. I've got an Indian on our squad who could probably beat you all alone."

That afternoon the Braves from Carlisle took over. Tewanima won two distance races, Welsh took the quarter and half-mile events, and Burd won the hammer throw and placed second in the discus.

Then came Bright Path, the greatest of them all. He started off by running third in the 100-yard dash. But then he won the high jump, the broad jump, the 16-pound shot, the discus throw, and the 120- and 220-yard hurdles for a total of six first places and one third. The Indians won the meet, 71 to 41.

It was a foregone conclusion that Jim would make the Olympic team and go to Stockholm. It was just a question of what events he would pick. Because he excelled at everything he did, Jim decided on both the pentathlon, of five events, and the 10-event decathlon. This meant that he would have to undergo the strenuous test of competing against a field of highly trained specialists in a total of 15 events.

In an exhibition of all-around athletic ability that has never been matched and never will be, the big Indian swept the pentathlon by winning four of the five events — the 200-meter dash, the 1,500-meter run, the broad jump, and the discus. He was third in the javelin. His score was twice that of his nearest rival's.

Then he went on to win the decathlon with four victories — the shotput, the high hurdles, the high jump, and the 1,500-meter run. He was third in the 100-meter dash, the discus, the pole vault, and the broad jump, and fourth in the javelin and the 400-meter run.

Thorpe is the only man to win both the pentathlon and the decathlon and since the pentathlon is no longer offered trackmen in the Olympics — it was dropped in 1928 — there will never be another double winner.

One of sport's most dramatic moments came at the conclusion of the Games when the magnificent Indian was presented to King Gustav V of Sweden. Standing on the victory pedestal before 40,000 onlookers, Jim was given a bronze bust of the king for his decathlon victory and a jeweled model of a Viking ship for his pentathlon triumph. Then King Gustav said with emotion,

"You, sir, are the greatest athlete in the world."

Jim grinned and replied, "Thanks, King."

Jim returned to the United States, a hero to all the nation. President Taft sent him a personal letter of congratulation. He was paraded up Broadway and heard the roars of thousands of admiring New Yorkers. Many offers to capitalize on his fame poured in — one was to appear in vaudeville for $1,500 a week — but Jim turned them all down. He was captain of the Carlisle football team and he wanted to return for his final season.

Again he was a whirlwind on the gridiron and again he made the official All-American team. If Jim had never done anything in sport but play football he would be hailed as one of the immortals. In more than 20 college games the indestructible Indian played every second, and never had a bad day.

Read what the *New York Times* said of him in reporting his performance against West Point on November 9, 1912. Here are some sample quotes: "Standing out was Jim Thorpe, recently crowned athletic marvel of the age. . . . At times the game itself was forgotten while the spectators gazed on Thorpe, the individual, to wonder at his prowess. . . . He simply ran wild. It was like trying to clutch a shadow. He went through the West Point line as if it was an open door; his defensive play was on a par with his attack and his every move was that of a past master. . . . Thorpe tore off runs of 10 yards or more so often that they became common. . . . He wormed his way through the entire Army team. Every cadet in the game had his chance, and every one of them failed."

One of the cadets who failed to stop Jim on the spectacular run just described was a slim-hipped young halfback named Dwight D. Eisenhower, known as Ike to his classmates.

The Army game was the high spot of Jim's football career. A few weeks later a Boston newspaper published a story in which he was charged with taking money for playing baseball while he was away from Carlisle. Confronted with the story, the honest Indian admitted that the charges were true. In his own defense, Jim said,

"I hope I will be partly excused by the fact that I was simply an Indian school boy and did not know I was doing wrong. . . . I was not very wise to the ways of the world."

Sportsmen all over the world were shocked at the revelations but most of them sympathized with Jim and hoped that he would be forgiven. But rules are rules and the Amateur Athletic Union decided that there could be no exception.

Jim was ordered to return his Olympic medals and trophies. His victories at Stockholm were stricken from the records. His medals were awarded to the men who had won second place, Bie of Norway in the pentathlon, and Wieslander of Sweden in the decathlon. Both refused the medals, saying, "We didn't win them. Thorpe did, no matter what your amateur rules are."

Crestfallen, Jim left Carlisle and spent the summers playing baseball, and in season professional football with the Canton Bulldogs. His major-league baseball career began with the New York Giants in 1913 and lasted for eight years, during which time he also played for the Reds and Braves as an outfielder.

He was never a stellar performer on the diamond because of his shortcomings as a hitter and his refusal to keep in training. Jim spent a lot of time on the bench, yet when he was used regularly he hit well.

In 1919, his last year in the majors, he played 60 games for the Braves and hit .327. However, his lifetime average is only .252.

Despite his mediocre baseball showing, Jim Thorpe remains the supreme athlete of all time. What other man has been twice an All-American football player, an Olympic double all-around champion, and a major-league baseball player?

In 1950, almost 40 years after Jim's golden days, the Associated Press conducted a poll of the nation's sports experts to select the greatest athletes of the first half of the twentieth century. Jim topped the list as the "Greatest Male Athlete," running far ahead of Babe Ruth, Jack Dempsey, Ty Cobb, Bob Jones, and Joe Louis. He was also named "Greatest Football Player," above such stars as Harold (Red) Grange, and Bronko Nagurski. On the "Greatest Track and Field Performer" list, Jim was second to Jesse Owens.

There will never be another one like Bright Path, the all-time greatest athlete.

Thorpe was a major league baseball player for eight years and one season hit .327.

Hannes Kolehmainen, the first of the Flying Finns, was Olympic distance running champion in 1912 and marathon winner in 1920.

CHAPTER 4

PAAVO NURMI, THE FLYING FINN

SUPERB AS JIM THORPE was at Stockholm in 1912, the Games did not wholly belong to him. Indeed, many thought that a loose-limbed runner from Finland named Hannes Kolehmainen turned in a performance that was just as amazing as the Indian's.

Kolehmainen, who stood a slim 6 feet, 6 inches and had a smooth, effortless stride, created a sensation at the Games by winning three distance races. He was first in the 5,000 meters, a distance of about three miles, which he covered in the world record time of 14 minutes 36.6 seconds. He won the grueling up-and-down cross-country run (about five miles), and then the 10,000 meters, which is a little more than six miles.

Some writers give Hannes credit for winning four races because he made the best time of the meet in the 3,000-meter team race, which is around two miles. However, he did not get a gold medal for winning the race in record time, nor was he credited with an official Olympic victory.

This unusual happening came about in the first heat of the 3,000-meter team race in which the United States was paired against Finland. Each country entered teams of five men. Hannes easily won his part of the race but this did not mean that the Finnish team had won. Unfortunately for Hannes, his four teammates did so poorly that the Finnish team as a whole did not score the points needed for a victory and, therefore, was eliminated by the American team.

Next day the United States defeated Sweden and Great Britain in the three-team final for the Olympic championship. The first man across the finish line was Tel Berna of Cornell, who had run far behind Hannes the day before. One cannot help but wonder what Hannes's thoughts were as he sat on the side lines and saw the man he had conquered so easily win a gold medal in time that was much slower than his own had been.

It is doubtful whether he was bothered much, for he was a fine sportsman who took his victories and defeats with grace. Not often was he beaten, though. In any race over a mile no one could stay with him. He was, in fact, the greatest distance runner the world had seen up to that time. His deeds were an inspiration to the youth of Finland and because of him the country eventually came forth with a cluster of track stars. Sports writers called them the Flying Finns and Hannes was the first of them.

At Stockholm the United States captured 16 of the 29 track and field events — counting Jim Thorpe's double triumph — but it was little Finland that won the admiration of the crowd. Smaller in population than New York City, the country sent only a handful of athletes to the Games, yet they won six gold medals, which was more than any other nation won except the United States. Even though half of them were won by the great Hannes, it was a remarkable showing for such a tiny country.

Among the thousands of Finnish boys who idolized Hannes upon his return from Stockholm was a 15-year-old lad named Paavo Nurmi, who lived in the city of Abo.

Paavo had not had a very happy childhood. At the age of 12, when his father died, he was forced to leave school and go to work. He did not have time to play games as other boys did, but he wanted to be an athlete. He decided to become a champion runner like Hannes Kolehmainen. Even as a boy he began to train hard and follow a strict program to develop stamina, speed, and condition. Almost every day the determined youngster would run behind suburban trolley cars mile after mile in order to develop an even, steady pace. This could not have been much fun, but Paavo did not care. He had his sights on the championship of the world and he knew that the road to the top was not an easy one.

The serious, dedicated boy grew up an unsmiling young man who spoke but few words. Rarely did he grin or show any sign of emotion.

The 1916 Olympics were not held because of World War I, but Paavo kept right on training with the 1920 Games in mind. They were held in Antwerp, Belgium, and for the first time the United States did not run away with the track and field events. This was because of the amazing Finns, who shared top honors with the United States in gold medals, each country winning eight of the 27 contests.

It was at these Games that Paavo, then 23 years old, began his great career. Clad in white trunks and a sky-blue T-shirt bearing the Finnish flag as an emblem, he ran with unsurpassed ease and grace. His running style was to become world-famous. His body erect, he strode with an even, flowing movement that never changed from start to finish. He was like a mechanical man. Indeed, he often carried a stop watch strapped to his wrist and consulted it at the start of every lap. He did not care what the other runners did, or how far ahead or behind they might be. He knew that the race could be won if he made a certain time, so he kept his eye on the watch and ignored his competitors. He ran against the watch, not men.

Although Paavo was beaten in his first Olympic race — he was nipped at the tape in the 5,000 meters and got second place — he came back to win the 10,000-meter run and led Finland's team to victory in the 10,000-meter cross-country. Meanwhile his countrymen were collecting medals in a variety of events, some of which had been largely American properties up to this time. The Finns won the running hop, step, and jump, the shotput, the discus, and the pentathlon. In the javelin throw, the greatest team scoring of the Games was done by Finland. Her four entries won the first four places. And in the marathon, which was the final event of the meet, old Hannes Kolehmainen gladdened the hearts of the crowd when he trotted into the stadium ahead of the field and circled the track to win in record time. Paavo, however, with two gold and one silver medal, was the outstanding performer of the Games.

His best was yet to come. Between Olympics, the expressionless Finn with the all-conquering will perfected his lap-by-lap speed controlled by his stop watch, and began demolishing world records. At almost every distance from 10,000 meters and six miles down to 1,500 meters and the mile, he made new world records, many of which had been standing for years.

After four years of hard competition against top-flight runners on tracks throughout Europe, Nurmi was ready for his greatest test — the 1924 Olympics at Paris. He now knew to a split second exactly what he could do to the limit of his endurance at any distance.

At Paris he decided to try something that no man had ever dared before — to win the 1,500 meters and the 5,000 meters on the same afternoon. Such a feat could be accomplished only by a superman, but Paavo was just that. Within 90 minutes the incredible Finn not only won both races but made Olympic records in both!

Then, two days later, as if to prove he was a superman, Paavo entered the 10,000-meter cross-country run. Under a broiling sun that forced 24 of the 39 starters to quit from exhaustion, the magnificent Finn strode like a well-oiled machine over fields, up and down hills, and over water jumps to win handily.

The next day, while several of his cross-country competitors were under medical care in the hospital, Paavo stepped up to the mark in the 3,000-meter race and led his country to victory in Olympic record time.

He now had won four gold medals, thus duplicating the performance of the American, Alvin Kraenzlein, in 1900. Paavo's triumphs were far more outstanding, however, because they were severe tests of endurance against a much wider field of competition.

Had it not been for Nurmi, the sports world would have acclaimed a fellow countryman of his named Willie Ritola as the hero of the 1924 Games. Ritola was one of the great Flying Finns, but he had the misfortune to come along when Paavo was at his best. He was the iron man of the Paris Games, winning the 10,000-meter run and the 3,000-meter steeplechase, and he ran second to Paavo in both the 5,000-meter and the 3,000-meter team race.

Although the United States won one more gold medal than Finland — 10 against nine on the 26-event program — the Flying Finns were supreme on the track at all distances over 800 meters, which is just a step or two short of half a mile.

Paavo came to the United States in 1925 to run on indoor tracks during the winter. Thousands of Americans packed arenas and ar-

Nurmi leads the field in the tough 10,000 meters
cross-country race at Paris, 1924.

Paavo Nurmi of Finland, the greatest distance
runner of all time.

mories to see him wherever he performed. Although he had never run on board tracks before, the Phantom Finn — as the press now called him — ran away from all American opposition and made world indoor marks almost every time he started. During the strenuous tour, which spanned the entire nation and allowed him little rest as he jumped from city to city, his only setback came when he ran a half-mile race. It was not his distance and he was beaten, but it took the half-mile champion, Alan Helffrich, to do it. Not even Nurmi was superman enough to be unbeatable at every distance.

His greatest achievement on the tour was his shattering of the two-mile record in New York on February 14, 1925. Making new marks was nothing new to the Phantom Finn, but this was something special because when he broke the tape in 8 minutes 58.2 seconds, he became the first human to run two miles in less than nine minutes. For years distance men had tried to get through the seemingly impossible nine-minute barrier. Nurmi's feat was as great as the lowering of the four-minute barrier in the mile a generation later.

In the Olympics at Amsterdam in 1928, Paavo was an old man athletically speaking, and his best days were behind him. Nevertheless, he won the 10,000 meters, defeating his old rival, Willie Ritola, and then placed second to Ritola in the 5,000 meters. Paavo acquired another silver medal by running second to Toivo Loukola, another of the Flying Finns, in the 3,000-meter steeplechase.

There were 22 track and field events on the slate at Amsterdam and the United States won eight gold medals to Finland's five. Canada and Great Britain each won two, and the remaining five went in singles to five different nations. After the Games American newspapers headlined:

WE WON THE OLYMPICS BUT THE FINNS BEAT US ALL HOLLOW

In a sense this was true, but it must be remembered that no country ever "wins" the Olympic Games because there is no scoring. The International Olympic Committee does not recognize any system of scoring and tries to discourage the press from making a tabulation. The press persists in doing this, but the tabulation is unofficial and therefore meaningless.

42

In the 10,000-meter flat race at Amsterdam, 1928. Edvin Wide of Sweden takes the lead, followed by Paavo Nurmi and Willie Ritola of Finland. The race was won by Nurmi, Ritola second and Wide third.

It could be said, though, that the United States made the best showing at Amsterdam in respect to the number of gold medals won. Yet it could also be said that the Finns did "beat us all hollow" because America won only one individual race. This was Ray Barbuti's victory in the 400-meter run. America's other victories were gained in the field events and relay races, but the Flying Finns, as usual, kept running and breaking tapes. Without question they did beat the Americans "all hollow" on the cinder track.

When Paavo closed his Olympic career in 1928, he had won a total of seven gold medals in three sets of Games. No other runner has ever lasted so long in the Olympics or has won so many championships.

The Finnish superman had everything — a fine, well-conditioned body, a strong will dedicated to victory, and a heartbeat so slow that doctors who examined him could scarcely believe their ears. The average man's beat is 72 per minute. Nurmi's was 40, one of the slowest ever recorded in a healthy man. The subnormal beat kept him from tiring quickly and helped give him his unbelievable stamina. Strict training did the rest.

Athletic greatness is judged by the number of championships a man wins in top-flight competition, the records he makes, and the number of years he stays on top. Nurmi was supreme in all.

He lasted nearly 15 years, during which time he was virtually unbeatable. He broke 13 world records, all of them at standard distances. Not counted here are the innumerable national, Olympic, and indoor marks he established against the world's best runners. It would take several pages to list them, but these are the distances at which he made *world* records: one mile, two miles, three miles, four miles, five miles, and six miles; 1,500 meters, 2,000 meters, 3,000 meters, 5,000 meters, 10,000 meters, and 20,000 meters (about 12 miles).

One more world mark, which, incidentally, stood for 17 years, was his one-hour run to see how much ground he could cover in that time. The distance was 11 miles and 1,648 yards, which is just 12 yards short of 12 miles.

One by one Nurmi's old marks have been broken, but it took many years and several runners to do it. Wider competition, improved tracks and equipment, and sounder training methods account for the gradual lowering of records in every field. It does not matter, however, that Nurmi's marks have been gradually bettered over the years, for his achievement remains unassailable. No other runner ever held as many records as he did, or was so supreme for so many years. If he were in his prime today, he would undoubtedly be cracking the four-minute mile and leaving everybody far behind in the longer races. Without any question, Paavo Nurmi was the greatest distance runner the world has ever seen.

44

CHAPTER 5

BABE DIDRIKSON, THE GIRL MARVEL

FOR CENTURIES the Olympic Games of ancient Greece were exclusively for the male sex. Women were forbidden by law to attend the Games or even to take a peek at them from the nearby hills. The penalty for the offense was death and the execution was carried out by hurling the lady off a cliff.

Pherenice, a widow of noble birth, was the first female who saw the Games and lived to tell about it. Her son, Pisidorus, was an Olympic runner who had been trained by his father. The father died while the youth was in training and Pherenice took over the task of preparing her son for the Games. When the day came for Pisidorus to race, Pherenice had such a desire to see him perform that she disguised herself as a man and walked into the stadium. To her great joy she saw him win his race, but she forgot her caution and filled the air with soprano shouts of elation. Then she rushed on to the field and kissed him. It was obvious to everybody that this was no man. Pherenice was arrested, tried, and found guilty. However, her plea of mother love was so strong that she won over the public, and her life was spared.

Eventually women were allowed to see the Games. Toward the last, when the Olympics were under Roman control, women were even permitted to compete, but only in the chariot races.

The ladies had their own set of Games, which were called the Heraea, in honor of Hera, the wife of Zeus. Every four years the

Marble statue of a Grecian Girl Runner of about 500 B.C.
Vatican Museum, Rome.

Heraea were held, sandwiched in between the Olympic Games. It is not known just when these Games began or ended, for no records have come down to us. It is believed, however, that they existed for several hundred years and petered out when Greece was absorbed by Rome.

The Heraea program was limited to foot races of short distances and the girls ran barefooted with their unbound hair streaming out behind them. They wore a short tunic which exposed the right shoulder and ended well above the knees. A statue of a Grecian Heraea runner of about 500 B.C. attired in this costume can be seen in Rome today.

In the second modern Olympic Games in 1900 women made their first appearance when six females took part in the then gentle game of lawn tennis. In the following Olympics, except for 1904, when there were no women's sports, their number gradually increased as more sports were added.

Archery and figure skating for women were introduced in London in 1908, swimming in 1912, and fencing in 1924. Figure skating for both sexes was shifted to the Winter Games when they came into being in 1924, and four years later at Amsterdam women competed in track and field sports for the first time.

In 1928 the United States sent a track and field team of 19 girls to Holland to compete with 24 nations in the five-event program, which consisted of the 100 and 800 meters, the high jump, the discus throw, and the 400-meter relay. In the Parade of Nations at the start of the Games the American girls in white ensembles with white felt hats and white shoes made a favorable showing as they marched around the stadium before 40,000 spectators.

America won its share of honors even though most of the women from the other nations had had many more years of competition than those from the United States. Elizabeth Robinson of Illinois, who broke the tape in the 100-meter dash, was America's only winner, but the Yankee girls took second in the discus and the relay, and third in the high jump. The Canadian team made the strongest showing with victories in the high jump and relay.

In the 800-meter race the girls staggered across the finish line in various stages of distress. It was obviously too long and exhausting a race for them and there was much unfavorable comment about it afterward. The event was dropped from the women's program shortly thereafter but was revived in 1960.

There was no outstanding woman performer in the 1928 Games but there was a star in the making at that time — a fourteen-year-old girl from Beaumont, Texas, who was even then in training for the next Olympics. She was Babe Didrikson, called Babe because she could hit a baseball a mile, just like Babe Ruth, or so her playmates said. Her real name was Mildred Ella Didrikson and she was born on June 26, 1914, the sixth child of Norwegian immigrants who had come to America a few years before.

Babe was a tomboy and looked it. A sharp-featured, jut-jawed girl with a straight, wiry figure, she could hold her own with the neighborhood boys in any of their games and do better than most. She was born an athletic genius.

"Before I was in my teens, I knew exactly what I wanted to be when I grew up," she wrote in her autobiography. "My goal was to be the greatest athlete who ever lived."

She first heard about the Olympics when her father read her newspaper stories of the Games in the summer of 1928. The inspired youngster said to him, "Next year I'm going to be in the Olympics myself." After it was pointed out to her that she would have to wait four years for the next Olympics, she vowed that she would start training right then and there for a place on the 1932 team. At that time she had never even seen a track meet, but she was fast and liked to jump over things like hedges and fences, and she had an urge to be first in everything she tried.

Babe was only 15 years old, not much more than five feet tall, and weighed only 105 pounds when, as a junior in Beaumont High School, she made the girls' basketball team. Most of the girls she played against were much bigger and taller, but Babe was fast, and ran right around them. From the very first game she was Beaumont's high scorer and at the end of the season was named on the all-city and all-state teams.

Babe made such a name for herself that she was offered a job by the Employers Casualty Company of Dallas, an insurance firm that sponsored athletic teams. It was understood that Babe would play on the firm's team while working as a clerk for $75 a month. This was the major league of women's basketball. The Employers Casualty

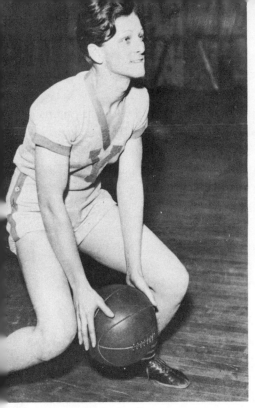

Left, Babe Didrikson, the All-American girl basketball player.
The Babe (second from right) breaks the tape to win by inches the
80-meter hurdle race in the Olympics in Los Angeles, 1932.

Company had developed some of the best players in the country and
every year its team took part in the United States national tournament.

Babe fitted in like a veteran her first year. She was the team's
dynamo, its high scorer, and after the national tournament was held,
she was chosen for the women's All-American basketball team. That
was in 1930. Next year Babe sparked the team that won the national
championship, and was again named All-American. In 1932 she won
that honor for the third year in a row.

Meantime, the energetic Babe was by no means idle when the
basketball season ended. Remembering her vow to make the Olympic
team, she persuaded her employers to start a track and field team. She
had seen a track meet by this time and was fascinated by the sport,
determined to try every event and be the best at all.

"I really worked hard at that track and field," Babe later recalled.
"I trained and trained and trained. I've been that way about every
sport I've taken up."

The two-hour afternoon practice sessions were not enough for her. At night she would go alone to the field and practice by herself until it got dark, which wasn't until nine o'clock on summer nights. If there was a good clear moon she kept going even longer, timing her step for the broad jump and the high jump. Then she would finish off by running the 440 yards as fast as she could.

Babe won her first national track honors in the summer of 1930 at the women's A.A.U. championships at Dallas. She won the javelin throw and the baseball throw and made a world record in the broad jump with a leap of 18 feet, 8½ inches. Her record lasted only a few minutes, however. She had hardly regained her feet when a lanky girl named Stella Walsh sailed off the mark and took first place away from Babe by jumping a fraction of an inch farther.

Remember the name, Stella Walsh, for she, too, was to become an outstanding track and field champion.

Next year the national championships were held in Jersey City and Babe was the leading scorer with three first places — the broad jump, the 80-meter hurdles, and the baseball throw, making a world record with a heave of 296 feet.

Then came the Olympic year, 1932, and Babe was keyed up as never before. The national A.A.U. championships and the Olympic tryouts were combined in one meet, which meant that those who won or placed high in the nationals would be put on the Olympic team.

Babe went to Chicago, where the meet was held that summer, as a one-girl track team, the sole representative of the Employers Casualty Company. There were over 200 girl contestants on the field. Some clubs sent 15 or more girls. The Illinois Women's Athletic Club had a team of 22. Babe stood by herself watching the various teams as they were introduced over the loud-speaker. When it came time to announce her "team" she stepped out in view and took a bow all alone. There was a great roar from the crowd. No one in the stands knew that the smiling, brown-haired girl they were looking at was going to make history that afternoon.

There were 10 individual events on the program and Babe was entered in eight. She was in everything but the 50-yard and 220-yard dashes. Two of the events she was going to try — the shotput and the discus — were new to her.

For almost three hours that afternoon Babe was rushing and

leaping all over the place. She would run a heat in a race, then she'd take one of her high jumps and follow it with a broad jump, a javelin throw, or a toss of the discus. She did not have a second's rest all afternoon.

When it was all over, the officials began adding up the points to determine the team standings. Soon they were looking at each other unbelievingly. Their sheets showed that Babe Didrikson had made more points than any team. She had a total of 30. In second place, with 22 points, was the Illinois Women's Athletic Club. It did not seem possible, but it was true. Babe had won the national championship singlehanded!

Of the eight events she entered she was shut out in only one, the 100-meter dash. She won five events outright: the shotput, baseball throw, javelin throw, broad jump, and 80-meter hurdles, and she tied for first place in the high jump. In the discus throw she was fourth.

Next morning people all over the country read the United Press story of the meet, which said that Babe had put forth "the most amazing series of performances ever accomplished by any individual, male or female, in track and field history." Babe woke up a national figure that morning.

Overjoyed because her dream of wearing the American shield in the Olympics had come true, Babe was nevertheless a little disappointed to find that she was not allowed to enter more than three events in the Games. She chose the javelin, the 80-meter hurdles, and the high jump. The other two events were the 100-meter dash and the 400-meter relay.

On Monday, August 1, 1932, Babe got the thrill of her life when she marched into the Olympic Stadium at Los Angeles at the opening of the Games as a member of the United States team. There was only one thing wrong with the ceremonies, Babe often recalled in later years. The white stockings she had to wear as part of the official uniform made her uncomfortable. It was the first time she had ever worn a pair of stockings in her life.

Babe felt better the next day in her old track shoes and socks. She picked up the javelin and hurled it 143 feet 4 inches for an Olympic and world record. Three days later she won another gold medal by taking the 80-meter hurdles in the Olympic and world record time of 11.7 seconds.

Stella Walsh, the Polish-born girl, was an all-around track star for nearly a quarter of a century. As a golfer Babe Didrikson Zaharias won more tournaments than any woman player in history.

Now all she needed to make a clean sweep of her three events was to win the high jump. Her great rival in this event was Jean Shiley, the girl who had equaled Babe's jump in Chicago a few weeks before for a first-place tie. Again the high jump turned into a contest between the two girls with the rest of the field eliminated. The cross bar moved up to 5 feet 5 inches, which was almost two inches higher than the record the girls had set in Chicago. Both cleared it. Now Babe had made world marks in all three of her events, but she had not won yet. There was still the jump-off of the tie to be settled.

The bar was moved up a quarter of an inch. Again both girls cleared it and it seemed as if the tie would never be broken. Then, suddenly, the judges announced that Babe's jump did not count. They ruled that she had dived over the bar head first, instead of feet first, as required by the rules of high jumping at that time. (This rule has since been discontinued.)

Babe was crushed. She protested that she had been jumping exactly the same way all afternoon — and all year, for that matter. The judges, however, would not change their decision. She had to be satisfied with second place.

In any event, the Yankee girls swept everything but the 100-meter dash. That sprint was won for Poland by Stanislawa Walasiewicz, a girl we have met before as Stella Walsh, which is her Americanized name.

The Polish-born girl was reared in the United States but represented her native country in the 1932 and 1936 Olympics. Although she was perhaps not so brilliant as Babe, the one-girl track team, she was almost as versatile, and certainly more durable. Stella lasted longer in championship competition than any other track and field athlete in history, man or woman.

In 1930, when she was 19, she won her first A.A.U. national championships, in the 100-yard and 220-yard sprints, and the broad jump. It is exceptional for sprinters to last more than seven or eight years — they lose their speed early — but Stella defied time and kept on and on. In 1948, 18 years after her first national triumphs, when she was 37, she won the same three championships again. Not yet finished, she kept going until she was past 40. In 1953 she was good enough to win the western regional pentathlon championship, a five-event contest. In all, she won about 40 United States national championships and world titles.

What a rivalry there would have been between Babe and Stella had the Texas girl decided to continue her track career! But Babe turned in her amateur card shortly after the 1932 Games and followed the dollar route. She went on vaudeville, played professional basketball and baseball (with the bearded House of David team), and generally exhibited herself around the country.

In 1935 she took up golf and, as in everything else she had ever tried, she was determined to become nothing less than the best in the world. Amazingly, that is exactly what she became — not only the best woman golfer in the world, but the best who ever lived.

Her first big title was the United States Women's National Amateur (she had been accepted as an amateur by the United States Golf Association) which she won in 1946. She followed that triumph with the British Women's Amateur title a lear later. It was her thirteenth consecutive tournament victory and, incidentally, the first time the British title had been won by an American woman.

That was just the beginning. Babe went on to win tournament after tournament and as a professional golfer — she left the amateur ranks for good in 1948 — she won three United States National Open Championships, four so-called World Championships, (the Tam-O-Shanter) and numerous other titles. If Babe had never tossed a basketball or pulled on a pair of track shoes, her name would stand high on the list of sports' immortals on her golfing achievements alone.

Awards were showered upon her. Five times the Associated Press voted her "Woman Athlete of the Year," the first time in 1932 for track, and four times as a golfer — in 1945, 1946, 1947, and 1950. In the mid-century poll which named the top athletes of the first half of the twentieth century, Babe stood alongside Jim Thorpe by winning the "Greatest Female Athlete" award. (Helen Wills Moody, the tennis champion of the twenties, took second place and Stella Walsh was third.)

Misfortune finally caught up with Babe. In 1953 she was told that she had cancer and must undergo an operation. Less than a year later the courageous girl was back on her feet, playing tournaments and making appearances for the American Cancer Society. More than anything else, she wanted to give hope to other cancer victims by showing them that the disease could be conquered.

In one of the greatest comebacks in the annals of sport, Babe took on the country's best women golfers in the 1954 National Open and, although she was weak and tired easily, won the championship — and by the margin of 12 strokes!

The greatest female all-around athlete of all time had only two years left after that blaze of glory. Soon she returned to the hospital. She died in 1956 at the age of 42.

CHAPTER 6

JESSE OWENS,
THE BUCKEYE BULLET

THE UNITED STATES continued its domination of the men's track and field at Los Angeles in 1932. Of the 23 events listed, the Yankees registered six track victories and five field championships, including the decathlon, for a total of 11 gold medals. Finland made the next best showing with three, Great Britain and Ireland won two each, and the remaining five went to five different nations.

The only double winner was Eddie Tolan, a chunky, bespectacled little Negro from Detroit. Eddie shared the headlines with Babe Didrickson by winning the 100- and 200-meter races and making Olympic records in both.

Superb though he was at Los Angeles, Eddie was soon to be overshadowed by another Negro track star who ran and leaped to world-wide fame in the mid-1930's. His name was Jesse Owens, and he was one of seven children in a poor family that had come from Alabama to Cleveland, Ohio, where Jesse grew up.

Jesse was born James Cleveland Owens, but when the youngster first went to school and was asked his name by the teacher, he gave the first two initials only, saying "J.C." The teacher heard it as Jesse and that is the way it is written in track's hall of fame.

Jesse was a shy, skinny boy with no inclination for sports. His name might have remained in obscurity if it had not been for a Cleveland high-school teacher who noticed the frail-looking lad one day and asked him to come out for track because he thought it would be good for the boy's health.

Jesse was not very enthusiastic about the sport. He trotted about on the cinder track with the other boys, only half interested in what he was doing. Then one day the track coach asked Jesse to run 100 yards in a time trial. When Jesse crossed the finish line the coach looked at his watch and said to himself, "This watch can't be right. It needs fixing." He had clocked Jesse in close to world-record time. The coach did not believe it until the jeweler, to whom he took the watch to be repaired, told him that it was in perfect working order. Thus did Jesse take his first flight to greatness.

Track coaches have a saying: "Sprinters, like poets, are born, not made." It is true that a boy who has no speed in his legs can never become a sprinter no matter how hard he practices. He can be shown how to improve his start, how to get off the mark more quickly, and perhaps a few things about running form. But no coach can inject speed into his legs if it is not already there. He has to be born with speed, and Jesse was a born sprinter.

He was unbeatable in high school and at Ohio State University, not only as a sprinter but also in the low hurdles and the broad jump. It was more than speed that made Jesse so remarkable, it was his versatility. Not since Alvin Kraenzlein, the sprinter-hurdler-broad jumper of 1900, had an athlete been so supreme in so many events. But Kraenzlein never had a day like one Jesse had, nor did any other track athlete, for that matter.

Jesse's day of days took place at Ann Arbor, Michigan, on May 25, 1935, when he was a 21-year-old sophomore at Ohio State. On that afternoon in the Big Ten Conference track meet, the 160-pound Negro was so astounding in his superiority and broke so many records that the 10,000 people who sat in the wooden stands at Ann Arbor could scarcely believe what they saw. Remember that Jesse was competing against the top athletes of several state universities from all over the Middle West.

Here is what Jesse did, step by step:
1. At 3:15 he sped down the track to win the 100-yard dash and tied the world record of 9.4 seconds. As usual, there were five yards of daylight between Jesse and the nearest man to him.
2. At 3:25 Jesse took his first and only broad jump and soared 26 feet 8¼ inches. He smashed the world record held by Chuhei Nambu of Japan by more than half a foot.

56

Jesse Owens, the great Negro all-around Olympic track and field star. *Below*, Jesse Owens on the mark in the 100-meter sprint at Berlin, 1936. The Ohio State marvel won four gold medals for the United States.

3. At 3:45 he flashed across the line in the 220-yard dash 10 yards in front of the field and shattered the accepted world record by three tenths of a second. His time was 20.3 seconds.
4. At four o'clock Jesse ended his one-man performance by flying over the 220-yard low hurdles in 22.6 seconds to take four tenths of a second off the previous world mark.

Three world records smashed and a fourth tied, and by one man in less than an hour! No other man, before or since, ever had such a day on any athletic field from the time the first Olympics were held in ancient Greece. The records Jesse shattered that afternoon represented the best efforts of the finest athletes from all over the world, and covered a period of many years. In one glorious hour Jesse wiped their names off the record books.

What made Jesse run so fast in that wonderful flowing style of his — so satin-smooth, it was said, that a cup of water could have been balanced on his head and he would not have spilled a drop?

Some claimed that he had a hidden physical advantage. A Cleveland doctor examined him. He X-rayed Jesse's leg bones, measured his arms, trunk, and legs, and declared that if Jesse had any advantage, he had attained it by superior training and courage.

Lawson Robertson, who coached the United States Olympic track team for many years, tried to explain the reason for Jesse's phenomenal speed. "Like all great sprinters, he has an abundance of nervous energy," said the coach, "and he has the finest pair of legs I have ever seen. The muscles are symmetrical and do not bunch. His legs are not ideal for sustained effort and perhaps they would not stand up well on a football field. But for speed and explosive effort, Owens' legs are perfect."

Jesse's perfect legs carried him to further glory in Berlin, where the 1936 Games were held.

Nazi Germany, then under the domination of Adolf Hitler, was eager to show the world that their leader had accomplished and staged the most stupendous Games ever seen. The Nazis built four magnificent stadiums, an outdoor theater, swimming pools, a polo field, and an Olympic village for male athletes that contained 150 cottages on beautifully landscaped grounds.

The gigantic Olympic stadium for track and field had a seating capacity of 110,000. Every day it was filled to the brim. Record crowds thronged the other stadia and arenas, where the swimming, soccer football, wrestling, boxing, fencing, weight-lifting, gymnastics, basketball, and other spectacles were held. In the whole Olympic area there was a total seating capacity of 237,000 and standing room for many more thousands. More than four and a half million tickets of admission were sold for the various sports. All during the Games the people turned out in vast numbers, more than ever before. An exhibition baseball game played by two amateur American teams drew the largest crowd that had ever attended a baseball game anywhere, including the World Series.

A record number of 5,300 athletes representing 52 nations met in Berlin at a time when a troubled world was seething with national hatreds and about to erupt into war. But there was no hatred among the athletes. Sportsmanship prevailed, national jealousies were put aside, and the Olympic Games fulfilled the vision of founder Baron Pierre de Coubertin. He was then 73 years old and had but three more years to live.

On July 21, eight days before the Olympics opened in Berlin, a group of Grecian girls attired in ancient costumes gathered at the original site of the Games in Olympia and ignited a fire with a lens and the sun's rays. They brought the sacred fire in an antique lamp to a square, where a runner with a magnesium torch stood waiting. The runner lit his torch from the lamp and then started off in the general direction of Berlin, 1,837 miles distant. He was the first of a relay of 3,300 runners each of whom ran half a mile and lit one torch from another. Night and day the youths sped across the land, through Greece, Bulgaria, Yugoslavia, Hungary, Austria, Czechoslovakia, and Germany.

At noon, on August 1, just as the opening Olympic ceremonies were ending in Berlin, the last torchbearer ran gracefully through the east gate of the stadium and out on to the red-clay track, leaving a trail of blue smoke behind him. Thunderous applause from 110,000 people greeted him. Then he raced up the steps to the top of the stadium and lit a fire in a marble basin that burned until the Games ended on August 16.

The best organized and most magnificent Games ever held were dominated by the "Tan Cyclone" from Ohio State, as sports writers called the incomparable Jesse Owens. He won his first gold medal in the 100-meter dash. Ordinarily Jesse was not a fast starter but this time he exploded from the mark at the crack of the gun. He led all the way, and when the tape hit him he was running as fast as any human being had ever run. They clocked him in 10.3 for an Olympic and world record but unfortunately this was later disallowed because of an aiding wind.

Jesse went on from there. He catapulted himself through the air to win the broad jump and made an Olympic mark of 26 feet 5$\frac{5}{16}$ inches. It was the first time anyone had ever jumped over 26 feet in the history of the Games. For the second time Jesse mounted the winner's platform and received a gold medal, an olive wreath, and a small potted oak tree as a living memorial of his victory.

Still to come was his greatest performance, the 200-meter sprint that was run around a turn. (The world record for this distance was then 20.6 seconds on the straightaway and 21.2 around a turn.)

It was the worst kind of day for making fast time on a running track. It was cold and blowy and rain began to fall as the shivering finalists took their places on the turn for the staggered start. Then the gun barked, and Jesse burst out in front with arms and legs working in perfect rhythm. At the halfway mark he led by two yards and was gliding along so smoothly that he hardly gave the impression of running. At the tape he was five yards in front. The clockers got him in 20.7 seconds, which was the fastest anyone had ever run the distance around a turn. No one had ever broken 21 seconds flat before except on a straightaway and Jesse came within a tenth of a second of equaling that mark.

Owens now had three gold medals but he was not yet finished. He helped win the 400-meter relay as lead-off man and the quartet set an Olympic and world record of 39.8 seconds, averaging better than 10 seconds per man for 100 meters.[1]

That made four gold medals for Jesse and he was in rare company. Only Paavo Nurmi and Alvin Kraenzlein had won that many in one set of Games. In many ways Jesse's achievement was the most remarkable because of the extremely keen competitions at Berlin. There were 893 track and field athletes entered (three times the number of competitors at Los Angeles) which necessitated many tiring

[1] No one has ever broken 10 seconds in the 100-meter sprint. However, relay runners have averaged under 10 seconds per man for the distance. This is because the three men who follow the lead-off man have the advantage of flying starts. When the baton changes hands, the runners are going full speed.

On the victory pedestal at Berlin in 1936 stands Helen Stephens, a Missouri farm girl who won the 100-meter dash. Second was Stella Walsh (fitting on olive wreath) and third was Germany's Kaethe Krauss.

preliminary heats. To win his four medals Jesse had to run the 100 meters four times, the 200 meters four times, the 400-meter relay twice, and make two broad-jump performances. During these 12 appearances he bettered or equaled the existing Olympic record nine times, the world mark four times. In the 100-meter dash he broke the world record three times but none of the marks was allowed because of a slight following wind. Of the 893 track and field athletes from 42 nations, Jesse was the only one who won more than one gold medal.

The United States captured 12 of the 23 track and field events, thus maintaining its superiority in the sport that is considered the most important in the Olympic Games. Still in evidence were the Flying Finns with three victories in the distance races. Germany, which had never before won a first place in the history of the Games, won three field events. Japan and Great Britain won two each and New Zealand one.

In the six-event women's program two victories went to the United States. Helen Stephens, a lanky Missouri farm girl, beat Stella Walsh in the 100-meter sprint by two yards and set an Olympic and world record of 11.5 seconds. Helen ran anchor on the 400-meter relay team and helped win this event for her country.

How much space would there have been between the two fastest humans, Jesse Owens and Helen Stephens, if they had met in the 100-meters? Based on Jesse's 10.3 and Helen's 11.5 she would have trailed by about 12 yards. Does that mean that women have never been in the same class with men as speedsters? Not quite. Helen's time at Berlin bettered by half a second the time made by Tom Burke when he won the 100-meter championship in the 1896 Olympics at Athens.

When Jesse came home, he received a hero's welcome, ticker tape and all. Soon after he turned professional. He became a stunt runner and raced against trucks and dogs and baseball players with a head start. In Havana he ran against a race horse — and won. He ran in France and Norway and England and Australia.

In 1951, on a gray August day, he stood once more in Berlin's Olympic Stadium, the scene of his greatest achievement. He was there in his track suit as part of a show arranged by the United States High Commission. More than 75,000 German citizens turned out to see him. In his address, Jesse urged them to "stand fast with us in the fight for freedom and democracy under the protection of the Almighty God."

The big crowd stood as one to pay him homage. Many who cheered him that day had cheered him in 1936. Then Jesse jogged around the track, still graceful, still very much an athlete, and disappeared into the chute leading to the dressing rooms.

CHAPTER **7**

THE KID FROM TULARE

WAR ENGULFED THE WORLD three years after the 1936 Games were held and so long and bitter was the struggle, so deep the hatreds between nations, that it did not seem possible the Olympics would ever be revived. But the Olympic flame refused to be put out. As soon as peace was declared, the International Olympic Committee held a meeting and awarded the Games to London, to be held in 1948.

The announcement of the renewal was hailed with great enthusiasm in most countries. People everywhere wanted to forget the sad and dreadful war and turn to more pleasant and friendly activities.

A brand-new crop of athletes seemed to appear out of nowhere — eager and fit young men and women who were mere children when the Games were last held. One of them, an American youngster, was a five-year-old toddler when Jesse Owens stood on the victory platform in Berlin.

He was Robert Bruce Mathias and he was born in Tulare, California, on November 17, 1930. Bob came by his athletic talents through his father, Dr. Charles M. Mathias, who played an end on the University of Oklahoma football team in the 1920's. The family moved from Oklahoma to California the year Bob was born.

When Bob was a growing boy it did not seem likely that he would ever get anywhere in athletics. At 14 he was a gangling 5 foot 10 and too weak and anemic to try out for any of the Tulare High School teams. Instead, he played trumpet in the school band. His doc-

Bob Mathias, the 17-year-old school boy who won the 10-event decathlon in the London Olympics in 1948.

tor-father kept dosing him with iron pills and his mother fed him the proper food for anemia, and gradually the good care began to have its effect on him.

Then suddenly he shot up, and his body became firm and muscular. He made the school football, basketball, and track teams, and by the time he was 17 he stood an even six feet and weighed 190 pounds. No one could feel sorry for Bob and more. He was extremely handsome with his deep blue eyes and square chin and wide shoulders. He had developed a magnificent physique and had made a name for himself as one of California's top high school athletes.

One day in 1948, after the 17-year-old youngster had won some medals in an interscholastic track meet, his coach, Virgil Jackson, suggested that he try the decathlon in an Olympic regional trial meet that was going to be held in California in three weeks.

"Why not?" replied Bob, although he had never pole-vaulted, broad-jumped, run a distance race, or thrown the javelin, and all of these events were included in the arduous 10-event decathlon.

"I'll teach you," the coach said. For three weeks Bob and his coach worked hard together. Then they went to the meet in Pasadena and to everyone's amazement Bob won the decathlon. He beat a field of older and more experienced club and college track men.

"He was very green and only 17," the coach later said, "but I had a funny hunch that Bob might take it. He was a great competitor, an awfully tough kid to beat."

Still ahead was the big meet to decide the make-up of the United States Olympic team. This was the national championships and the Olympic finals combined in one meet. It was held in Bloomfield, New Jersey, and Bob crossed the continent to take part in it.

Competing against him were the finest athletes in the country, and no one was as young as Bob or as physically immature. Among his rivals was New York University's Irving Mondschein, who had won the national decathlon championship three times — in 1944, 1946, and 1947.

If Bob's performance at Pasadena was unbelievable it was more so at Bloomfield. Again he took top honors and thereby won a place for himself on the Olympic team. A few days later he sailed for London, the baby of the team, the youngest American ever to wear an Olympic track suit.

More exhausting by far than any test in the Olympic Games is the strenuous decathlon which requires one man to perform all the duties of an entire track team. The events are totally different and each one demands special skills. They are as unrelated as baseball, boxing, and rowing. Consider, for instance, the vast difference between such wide-apart events as the pole vault, the 1,500-meter run, the discus throw, and the high hurdles.

The change from one event to another in actual competition is sudden and jarring — as if an oarsman after a hard race jumped out of his boat and took to the tennis courts for three fast sets of tournament play.

Scoring is based on a complicated point system. The closer a competitor comes to equaling the world record in each of the 10 events, the more points are awarded to him. It is not so much whether he outruns or outjumps his rivals but rather how fast he runs and how high he jumps in relation to the best times and distances ever recorded. The man with the highest total for the 10 events is the winner.

Heavy penalties are imposed against mediocre and poor performances. A contender must be excellent in every event, for a single weakness will defeat him. He must have unlimited stamina and versatility, and he must be swift, strong, skillful, and consistent.

According to the Olympic rules the decathlon must be completed in two successive days. It is run off in this order:

First day: 100-meter dash, broad jump, 16-pound shotput, high jump, and 400-meter run.

Second day: 110-meter high hurdles, discus throw, pole vault, javelin throw, and 1,500-meter run.

In London on August 5 — less than three months after Bob had his first lessons in pole vaulting and javelin throwing — a field of 28 ambitious athletes representing 20 nations began competition in the first five events. There were so many contestants that they could not all start at the same time. It was necessary to divide them into two groups and start them one after the other. The second group had to wait until the first was finished and this meant that half of the field would not be through until long after dark. It was a decided handicap.

Bob Mathias had the bad luck to be in the second group, while all of his chief rivals were in the first. Furthermore, the day was gloomy and it rained most of the time. Despite everything, however,

All-around Bob Mathias (nearest camera) did everything well. Here he skims over the high hurdles.

the boy from Tulare gave a good account of himself during the long, exhausting first day, which began at 10 o'clock in the morning and lasted until 8 o'clock at night.

Bob did not win a single event outright but he tied for first place in the high jump with 6 feet 1¼ inches, and he was up with the leaders in the other four events. He went to bed that night completely worn out, yet so tense that he could not sleep. He stood third among the world's greatest decathlon men.

The next day London was a sea of rain, fog, and mud. It was the worst day in the history of the Olympic Games. All day it rained hard and for more than 12 hours Bob was on the field, huddled under a blanket which he would cast aside when he had to compete. His food consisted of two cold box lunches but he was too tired to eat the second one in the evening.

He had to pole-vault in half-light with a slippery pole, and by the time his turn came to throw the javelin it was so dark that he could not see the take-off line. Officials held a flashlight on it. Still remaining was the final event, the tough 1,500-meter run. It was after 10 o'clock and the only light came from the stands, where no more than a handful of people remained in the rain.

Bob had done better than ever the second day, and he knew as he took the mark in the last race that he was far ahead of the field. All he had to do now was to finish the race in fair time and he would win the decathlon.

Bob crossed the line and flopped wearily into his father's arms, then kissed his mother and said, "I wouldn't do this again for a million dollars."

Standing there on the victory steps as "The Star-Spangled Banner" was played, Bob became the youngest athlete ever to win an Olympic track and field championship. Afterward, when he was asked what he did to celebrate his fantastic victory, the likable youngster winked and replied, "I started shaving."

In all, he ran up a total of 7,139 points and was the only competitor to surpass the 7,000-point figure. Although he won only one event — the discus throw with 144 feet 4 inches — and tied in the high jump and pole vault (at 11 feet 5¾ inches), he did well in all the other events and never once faltered.

For the first time in Olympic history there was no double winner in men's track and field. There were some fine performances, though, and an upset that caused many a head to wag in wonderment.

The upset involved Harrison "Bones" Dillard, a string-bean of a Negro who got his nickname because of his long, lanky build. Bones came from Cleveland and his boyhood hero was Jesse Owens, who lived in the same city. The skinny youngster wanted to be a sprinter like Jesse but his high-school coach advised him to try the hurdles. So Dillard became a hurdler and, as time went on, a great one — perhaps the best the world had seen up to that time.

By the time he enrolled in Baldwin-Wallace College he was a full-grown track star, unbeatable in the hurdles. Over a period of 13 months before the 1948 Games, Bones ran the high and low hurdles on tracks all over the country, indoors and outdoors, at distances from 60 yards to 220 yards, and no one ever finished in front of him. In that time he compiled the almost unbelievable record of 82 consecutive victories. It is doubtful whether any track man ever won so many races in a row in major competition. His victories included conference, national and intercollegiate championships, and he held world records at various distances.

However, even the greatest athletes have days when everything goes wrong, and Bones had the misfortune to have his off day when it counted most — the day the Olympic tryout finals were held.

As he took the mark in the 110-meter high hurdle final it was a foregone conclusion that he would win the race and go to London and win the Olympics. Then it happened! Bones struck the second hurdle, swerved, lost his timing, and after floundering badly over a couple of more hurdles, quit in disgust. Instead of making it 83 straight victories, he not only lost the race but failed to win a berth on the Olympic team.

But wait! Bones was not quite finished. For some reason he had entered himself in the 100-meter dash. Bones, of course, was fast as all great hurdlers must be, but he was not considered to be on a plane with such speed merchants as Mel Patton, holder of the world record for the 100-yard dash (9.3 seconds), or Barney Ewell, recent conqueror of Patton, also a record holder and three times national sprint champion.

No one expected the heartbroken Clevelander to qualify in the short sprint, but Bones was determined to make up for his failure in the hurdles. By a superb effort he just managed to squeeze in as the third man on the team. He made it "on a rain check," one writer commented. So Bones sailed to London and wore the United States shield on his track suit — as a sprinter, not as a hurdler.

In the Olympic 100 meters 68 sprinters were entered. In order to reduce the field to the six finalists, it was necessary to run off 12 preliminary heats, four second-round heats, and two semi-finals. Through it all Bones hung on, qualifying every time, and when the big day came, the day of the Olympic final, there he was on the mark alongside Mel Patton, the California flash, and Barney Ewell, the Negro veteran from Penn State College.

The gun went off, and far on the outside in the sixth lane was Bones, off like a rocket. On the inside lanes Ewell and Patton were next to each other locked in a fierce struggle for what they understandably thought would mean the championship. They gave no thought to Bones far on the outside, nor did they see him.

As Ewell crossed the finish line with a lunge, he knew he had beaten Patton and was certain that he had nipped the field. He could not contain himself in his joy. He danced up and down and beamed widely — but hold on. Something was wrong. The judges were hailing Dillard as the winner. Poor Ewell's grin died suddenly when he realized that, sure enough, old Bones had won the race and there was no mistake about it. The world's greatest hurdler, who had failed in his specialty, had achieved the most dramatic upset of the entire Games.

Mathias and Dillard. The two names stood out above all others at London — the boy wonder and the man who came back. Those were the two they talked about, but there was another track and field genius on the scene at the time who turned in a truly incredible performance.

This athlete was not a man, though. She was a blond 30-year-old Dutch housewife and the mother of two children. She was Fanny Blankers-Koen.

The "Marvelous Mama" from Holland, as American sports writers called her, must go down in history as the greatest all-around woman track and field athlete who ever lived. Babe Didrikson excelled in a greater variety of sports and the durable Stella Walsh lasted longer as a track star, but no other woman has ever come close to the fair-haired Fanny as an all-around performer on the cinders, and it is doubtful whether anyone will ever equal her 1948 Olympic achievement.

When Fanny came to London, she held world records in both the high jump and the broad jump, but she decided not to enter these events. Since Olympic contestants are limited to three individual events, Fanny decided to try the two sprints — the 100 meters and the 200 meters — and the 80-meter hurdles, and run anchor on the Dutch 400-meter relay quartet. (A relay race is not considered an individual event.)

The Marvelous Mama was true to her nickname. She won the short sprint in 11.9 seconds, the 200 meters in 24.4 seconds, and the 80-meter hurdles in 11.2 seconds for a world record. Then as anchor on the 400-meter relay team she won her fourth victory. Thus the Dutch flier became the first and only woman to win four gold medals in one set of Games, and the fourth person to achieve such an honor.

Mrs. Fanny Blankers-Koen, the "Marvelous Mama" of Holland and mother of two children, is shown here winning the 80-meter hurdles in London, 1948. Fanny won four gold medals at London, the most ever won by a woman.

Customarily the Olympic Games are opened by the King or President of the host nation. Here, the late King George VI, views the parade of the athletes at London, 1948.

The other three, as noted before, were Kraenzlein, Nurmi, and Owens. Fanny's place is secure among the titans of the Olympics.

Forty years had elapsed since the Olympics were last held in London, and what a difference there was between the two sets of Games! Remember how the 1908 Games were marred by constant bickering and ill-feeling between America and Britain? It was just the opposite forty years later.

A statement to the British press by an American spokesman for the United States team as the Games ended contained this message of gratitude: "In no Olympic Games have we had a display of better sportsmanship or more comraderie. We thank Great Britain . . . and we want to express to the world our appreciation of the courtesy, fine feeling, and international good will which the Games brought to us."

There was, however, one unfortunate mix-up owing to a bad call by an official. The incident would probably have resulted in a serious flare-up had it taken place back in 1908, but sportsmanship and understanding prevailed in 1948 and there was no bitterness between the cousin nations.

It happened on the last day of the Games in the running of the 400-meter relay final before a sell-out crowd of 83,000. The American speedsters, Barney Ewell, Lorenzo Wright, Bones Dillard, and Mel Patton, were expected to beat the British quartet — and they did. Patton, running anchor, crossed the finish line a full six yards ahead of the field. Then, while the Americans were cavorting in joy over their victory and slapping each other on the back, the bad news came down like a thunderbolt! The American team was disqualified, it was announced. A judge had ruled that Ewell had handed the baton to Wright outside of the legal passing zone.

While the Yankees stood stunned, the British lads mounted the victory pedestal and the band played "God Save the King." It was Britain's first and only track and field victory. The British had been thirsting for a championship all during the Games and here it was at last. Yet in a fine display of sportsmanship the British crowd gave a far greater ovation to the disqualified Americans than to their own team which, after all, had not won a clear-cut victory.

The affair did not end there, by any means. The Americans formally protested the ruling. The Olympic Jury of Appeal made a careful study of the official movies of the race and came to the conclusion that the exchange of the baton had been perfectly legal, and the judge had been wrong. Later, the movies were viewed by millions of people and it was obvious to everyone that there had been no passing of the baton outside of the proper chalk marks.

Two days after the event it was announced that the United States team had won the relay. By this time almost everyone felt sorry — not angry — about the whole thing. The band "unplayed" "God Save the King," as it were, and played "The Star-Spangled Banner" instead. The four Britons had to give up their gold medals to the Americans, and the silver medals that Italy had been given were pried loose and presented to the Britons. Then the Hungarians had to give up their third-place bronze medals to the Italians. It was a mess all down the line but there was no ill-feeling about it. So ended the 1948 Games, on a high note of sportsmanship despite the relay incident.

The American men's track team made its usual fine showing with 11 victories out of the 24 events listed. Not so the Yankee girls. The only thing they won was the high jump, by Alice Coachman of Georgia, who leaped 5 feet 6½ inches for an Olympic record.

1948 (London) –
HARRISON DILLARD,
a hurdler by trade, fails
to make the USA team
in his specialty,
astounds by
capturing
the 100-
meter
dash
!

CHAPTER 8

STARS OF THE FIFTIES

IT IS STRANGE TO THINK of anyone as a seasoned veteran, an old-timer, at the age of 21, but that's what Bob Mathias was when he trotted out on the field at Helsinki, Finland, in 1952 to defend his Olympic decathlon championship.

Much had happened to the young man since he had last put on a United States track suit. He had become a crack fullback at Stanford University (he played in the Rose Bowl in 1951) and he had won the United States decathlon championship four times. Bob was the first man in American track history to win the event that number of times.

No longer was he the immature and at times gawky lad. He now stood 6 feet 3 inches and weighed 205 pounds, an increase of three inches and some 15 pounds since his London appearance. He was bigger and stronger than ever, and he had lost none of his speed or versatility.

In the summer of 1952 in the Olympic trials, Bob established a world record in the decathlon while qualifying for the team, and in so doing broke his own world mark which he originally set in 1950. As if that was not enough, the tremendous athlete did it again at Helsinki in gaining his second Olympic championship. This was Bob's farewell to the decathlon and it was a magnificent one. He was the first man in history to win two Olympic decathlon titles.

Inevitably his 10 performances in the event were compared to Jim Thorpe's. On paper it would have been no contest between the two men. Bob did better than Thorpe in every event except the 1,500-

meter run. It must be remembered, though, that such a comparison means next to nothing. Who can say what the Indian might have done under modern conditions? Bob himself fully realized this when he graciously (and truthfully) said of the great Indian: "If Jim Thorpe had the same coaching, track equipment, and competition as I have, I would hesitate to say that I could beat him."

Bob was not the only victor at London who won again at Helsinki. There was Mal Whitfield, an Army Air Force sergeant from Ohio State University, who ran with flawless form at London and won the 800-meter race in the Olympic record time of 1 minute 49.2 seconds. Then four years later, after he had married and had flown 27 bomber missions in Korea as tail gunner, Mal put on his track suit, went to Helsinki, and won the same race again in exactly the same time.

Still another repeater was the 100-meter champion at London. Remember Bones Dillard, the sprinter? Well, here he was again four years later, but this time he was Bones Dillard, the hurdler, aged 29. The Baldwin-Wallace graduate at last accomplished what he had set out to do in 1948, which was to win the Olympic high hurdles. Bones skimmed over the hurdles like a runaway deer to win by an eyelash and make an Olympic record of 13.7 seconds. A great competitor was old Bones.

The outstanding performer of the 1952 Games, however, was a 29-year-old Czechoslovakian army captain named Emil Zatopek, who was so superior as a distance runner that he almost made people forget the once-incomparable Paavo Nurmi.

The frail-looking Zatopek first made a name for himself at London by winning the 10,000 meters to become the first Czech ever to win an Olympic championship, and by running a very close second in the 5,000-meter race.

Oddly, Zatopek had wretched running form, perhaps the worst ever seen on the cinders. He ran with his head rolling about, his arms waving, and with a look of intense pain on his features. He would grimace, gnash his teeth, and gulp as he plodded gracelessly onward.

"He runs like a man who has just been stabbed in the heart," commented one sports writer. "Yes, he does everything wrong but win," said another. The writers nicknamed him the "Beast of Prague," so grotesque was his style.

For the second time Bones Dillard stands on the victory pedestal, but not for winning the 100-meter dash as he did in 1948. This time, in 1952 at Helsinki, he won the 110-meter hurdles. Standing with him for an all-American sweep are Jack Davis, second, and Arthur Barnard, third.

On the final lap of the 5,000-meter run at Helsinki, Emil Zatopek, the Czech, takes the lead and is trailed by Alain Mimoun, the French Algerian. Far back on the cinders is the fallen Chris Chataway of Great Britain.

For all his awkwardness, the Czech ran at a killing pace and always had so much in reserve that he did not seem human. The Finns, who were used to seeing among their own countrymen the greatest distance runners in the world — men like Kolehmainen, Ritola, and Nurmi — could not believe their eyes when they saw what Zatopek did at Helsinki.

Here is what he did: In the 10,000-meter grind (roughly six miles), he stayed well back for the first few laps, as was his custom, then at the sixth lap put on a labored sprint and took the lead. With him went Alain Mimoun, an Algerian representing France who had run second to Zatopek in the same race at London. Behind these two leaders trailed 29 men. Mimoun continued his close chase until the 18th lap when the Czech decided to get rid of him — and he did, by the astonishing margin of 50 yards in two laps. Zatopek was pouring it on like a sprinter when he crossed the finish line 320 yards in front of Mimoun.

The pace was so swift that it had to be a record and the clockers soon announced that it was. The Czech's time was 29 minutes 17 seconds, which was not only a record but a full 12 seconds faster than his own Olympic mark set at London four years before. In fact, the first six runners broke Zatopek's 1948 record.

Next for Zatopek was the 5,000-meter run. Gaston Reiff of Belgium, who had nosed out the Czech in this race at London, was among the 15 finalists and as defending champion he was determined to whip his rival again. But the pace was too much for the Belgian and at the 12th lap he dropped out, exhausted. Zatopek had plenty of opposition, however. Herbert Schade of Germany had set an Olympic mark in his qualifying round and in the final he led the race most of the time. Mimoun, the consistent plodder, was another dangerous contender.

As the runners started out on the last lap, the grimacing Zatopek, who looked as if he had just swallowed some poison, floundered ahead with a sprint. Right with him, though, went the gritty Mimoun and Schade. In the backstretch the men were bunched, and now it was anyone's race. For a moment Zatopek wavered, lost the lead for several seconds, and then, as if infuriated, he exploded past the front runners and staggered into the tape four yards ahead of Mimoun, who just managed to beat Schade.

This was Olympic record number two for Zatopek. His time of 14 minutes 6.6 seconds shattered the old Olympic mark by more than 10 seconds.

On the last day of the meet the fantastic Czech announced that he was going to run the marathon, a distance of 26 miles 385 yards. This race was new to him and he was not given much of a chance to win it. The uphill and down-dale course over pavements and dusty roads, totally unlike the level cinder path of the running track, was something that Zatopek had never before experienced.

The race started and ended in the Olympic stadium with miles of countryside in between. For the first 10 miles the Czech stayed back, content to let Jim Peters of Britain set the pace. At about the end of the 11th mile Zatopek began to take command. Soon he was leading and setting a faster pace than ever before. By the 20th mile he had killed off Peters and by the time the stadium was in sight, he had killed off 12 more runners. Behind him as he trotted through the gates of the stadium were 52 pursuers, but not one of them was in sight. The nearest man was almost half a mile in the rear.

For once the magnificent Czech ran smoothly and even grinned as he neared the finish line. He broke the tape, then casually strolled down the track, embraced his wife, and chatted with some friends for a few moments. He wasn't a bit out of breath! When the second place runner finally entered the stadium, Zatopek was munching an apple. "The marathon," observed the winner, "is a very boring race."

His time amazed everyone. The Czech ran the distance in 2 hours, 23 minutes and 3.2 seconds, which was just 6 minutes and 16 seconds faster than an Olympic marathon had ever been run before.

That was the third gold medal for Zatopek and his third Olympic record, and he had accomplished it all in seven days. His three championships were more than any country earned except the United States, whose team won 13 of the 24 events.

One more gold medal went to a Zatopek, but not to Emil. His wife won it in the javelin throw in the women's track and field. Thus the Zatopeks took back four gold medals to Czechoslovakia when the Games ended. This was the first husband-and-wife Olympic gold medal pair. Sports writers called the smiling couple, "Czech and double Czech."

At Helsinki there were new standards set in attendance and in number of athletes and nations represented. Present at the highly successful Games were 4,925 contestants from 69 countries, an all-time high figure.

Four years later at Melbourne, Australia, the site of the 1956 Games, there was a slight falling off in the number of Olympians — 3,539 athletes, 67 nations — due to the difficulties and expense of traveling to far-off Australia. However, for sheer drama and record-breaking performance and for all-out crowd enthusiasm and standing-room-only attendance, nothing had ever been seen like the Melbourne Games. The stadium with a capacity of 103,000 was filled for eight straight days of track and field competitions.

The conditions could not have been much worse. It was cold and windy almost every day. The brick-red surface of the new running track was soft and had a tendency to loosen up whenever track shoes

Vladimir Kuts of Russia wins the 10,000-meter run at Melbourne, 1956, all by himself in Olympic record time.

dug into it and it was the wrong time of the year for a track meet, according to many coaches and experts. The Games were held in November and December, which is Australia's spring. Never before had they been staged below the equator, where the seasons are reversed. Many thought that this would have a bad effect on the American and European athletes because they were used to training and performing in the northern spring and summer, from May to September. Then, too, many of the athletes were students who would have to leave college during the fall semester.

Despite everything — the horrible weather, the poor track, and the topsy-turvy season — five world records fell, and Olympic marks were set in 17 out of the 24 men's track and field events, and another one was tied.

No single athlete dominated the Games as Emil Zatopek had four years previously, but there were two double winners, a Russian and an American, and both set Olympic records.

It would be difficult to find two more different persons than Vladimir Kuts, the Soviet distance runner, and Bobby Joe Morrow, the American sprinter, who came together at Melbourne from opposite ends of the earth.

Kuts, the Soviet hero, came from an obscure village named Sumskaya in the Ukrainian wheat belt; Morrow, the American hero, was from San Benito, a small town in the Texas cotton lands. In physical appearance, running form, and personality they were as far apart as they were geographically. Kuts was short, solid, and unsmiling (except when he won), and had a peasant's broad face. He was built like an oak stump and had heavy, muscular legs. His long, corn-yellow hair kept flopping up and down as he ran, as if to keep time with his plodding mechanical-man stride. He was 29 years old and an officer in the Russian Navy.

Bobby Morrow, friendly and smiling with handsome, clear-cut features, was a 21-year-old student at Abilene Christian College in Texas and the son of a well-to-do cotton farmer. He stood a beautifully proportioned 6 feet 1½ inches and wore his reddish-brown hair closely cropped. His lithe frame was covered with long, rippling muscles and when he ran it was all grace and smoothness, as if he were gliding down the track on air.

Such was the difference between the double champions. Yet they were alike in many ways, for both had the common qualities of great determination, a will to win, and the ability to rise to tremendous heights under the terrific pressure of Olympic competition — qualities that all super-performers seem to have.

Track experts almost to a man thought that the marks set by the tireless Zatopek at Helsinki would stand up for years, perhaps for generations, but they hadn't yet seen Kuts. On a soft track the Soviet marvel fractured Zatopek's records in both the 5,000- and 10,000-meter races and while doing it, ran into the ground the finest group of distance men the Olympics had ever seen. Kuts simply killed off his adversaries one by one.

In the 10,000 meters he was the winner by 45 yards and was smiling and waving a hand to the crowd as he crossed the finish line in the Olympic record time of 28 minutes 45.6 seconds. He took more than half a minute off Zatopek's old mark. This was the first final event on the Olympic program. Five days later, after three preliminary heats had been run to reduce the field in the 5,000 meters, Kuts faced 13 rivals in the final. Three of the runners, Gordon Pirie and Chris Chataway of Great Britain, and Germany's Herbert Schade, had placed in the first six at Helsinki. In addition, Kuts, Chataway, and

Bobby Morrow, anchor man on the United States 400-meter relay team at Melbourne, takes the baton from Thane Baker and sprints ahead to victory. Having won the 100- and 200-meter dashes, Bobby won his third gold medal in the relay race.

Pirie had held world marks for the distance. With such a brilliant field there was bound to be fireworks — and there were.

The Britons planned to team up against Kuts and try to wear him down, or at least keep him from running away. But the Soviet star would have none of it. He set a blazing pace from the start and just kept it up. The Britons tried valiantly to stay with him but they began to fade at the halfway mark. Kuts continued to pile on the pace, adding four seconds to his lead at every lap and at the finish he was 80 yards in front. Even so, the first five men broke Zatopek's Helsinki mark. Kuts lowered it by 27 seconds with a stunning 13:39.6.

The double winner was the first Russian male track and field victor in Olympic history. Russia had sent a sizable team to Helsinki in what was the country's first real Olympic appearance[1] but the men failed to gain a single gold medal in track and field. Kuts more than made up for his country's poor showing at Helsinki.

On the same slow track Bobby Morrow, who had been off form because of a muscle injury, survived three 100-meter heats to reach the final. Then, against a strong, gusty wind he won by a yard in the fast time of 10.5 seconds. Bobby had twice tied the Olympic 100-meter mark of 10.3 seconds in the trial heats, but the stiff breeze in his face in the final cost him a fraction of a second.

"I don't care about the time," said the happy Texan. "I just wanted to win."

Winning the 200 meters was something else, though. There was no 200-meter straightaway at Melbourne so the sprinters had to start on a curve. Although Bobby was a magnificent curve runner and the staggered start did not particularly bother him, nevertheless he was seized with butterflies in the stomach. So badly did he shake that he nearly fell off his starting blocks.

"It was the thought of that second gold medal," he said later. "I kept seeing it so much that I couldn't even sleep."

Perhaps, too, Bobby was thinking of the two crack American dash men who were in the final against him. One was Andy Stanfield, a Seton Hall graduate who had won the 200 meters at Helsinki; the other was Thane Baker of Kansas State College, who had run second to Stanfield in the 1952 Olympics.

[1] Russia sent a limited number of contestants to the Games of 1908 and 1912 and won a total of four silver and three bronze medals in wrestling, yachting, and shooting; none, however, in track and field. Russia did not compete again until 1952.

Despite his attack of nerves, Bobby got off well and once the runners came out of the curve into the straightaway he was a few inches ahead of the field.

"We were all about even when we rounded the curve," said one of the runners in the dressing room after the race. "Now, I thought, we'll find out who's got it. We found out all right. That doggone Morrow just went zoom and the race was over."

Bobby's time was 20.6 seconds, a 10th of a second faster than the Olympic record that Jesse Owens had made in 1936 and Stanfield had equaled in 1952. No other man had ever run the distance faster around a curve. For such a soft track the time was astonishing. Stanfield ran second and Baker third. By winning Bobby became the first double-sprint victor since Owens 20 years earlier at Berlin.

The Texas powerhouse was not yet finished, though. As anchor man on the 400-meter relay team, the incomparable Morrow ran a sizzling race to help his teammates to victory. Despite one poor baton pass, which cost the team a fraction of a second, the quartet broke a world and Olympic record. The time was 39.5 seconds, replacing a mark that had endured for 20 years. Bobby went home to Texas for Christmas with three gold medals.

With all kinds of marks being shattered on the running track, there were two American athletes who meanwhile were establishing themselves on the field as consistent winners and record breakers.

One of the pair was W. Parry O'Brien, absolute king of the world's shotputters and the first man in history to throw the big iron 16-pound ball more than 60 feet. The gigantic University of Southern California graduate, who towered 6 feet 3 inches and weighed 238 pounds, had won his first Olympic championship at Helsinki with a toss of 57 feet 1½ inches. This bettered the previous mark by more than 11 inches.

Between Olympics Parry practiced and competed constantly and in 1954 broke through the mythical 60-foot barrier with 5¼ inches to spare. At Melbourne the consistent O'Brien broke his 1952 Olympic mark by a couple of inches on his very first throw, but that was just a warmup. Before he had finished he hurled the ball 60 feet 11 inches for an Olympic record and his second gold medal.

Parry went on to further triumphs after the Melbourne Games and eventually got over 63 feet. The good-natured, blue-eyed giant received the coveted James E. Sullivan Memorial Trophy in 1959.

An American Olympic champion at London in 1948 and at Melbourne four years later was shotputter Parry O'Brien, a world record holder.

Another London and Melbourne winner was the Reverend Robert E. (Bob) Richards, minister of the Church of the Brethren, and known as the "Vaulting Vicar."

The selection is made by sports authorities in a nationwide poll and is annually awarded to the "amateur athlete who does most to advance good sportsmanship during the year."

The other invincible American athlete on the field at Melbourne was the Reverend Robert E. (Bob) Richards, 30-year-old minister for the Church of the Brethren, whose pole-vaulting career went back to 1948. That year the "Vaulting Vicar," as the press dubbed him, won a bronze medal for third place at London, but by the time the Helsinki Games were held he had become the world's leader in his specialty. The 5-foot-10-inch University of Illinois graduate hoisted his 160 pounds over the bar at Helsinki to make an Olympic mark of 14 feet 11¼ inches.

The vicar was something more than a vaulting specialist, however. He was an accomplished all-around athlete and good enough to win the United States decathlon championship three times — in 1951, 1954, and 1956.

At Melbourne the veteran vaulter, now married and the father of three children, got the jolt of his life before he reached the final. Bob had cleared 15 feet more often than any man who ever lived, perhaps 100 times. Yet at Melbourne, when the bar was at the relatively small height of 13 feet 1½ inches in a preliminary round, he knocked it off as he went over it. Field competitors are allowed three tries before being eliminated and Bob was not particularly worried about his initial failure. Just a mishap, he thought. A few minutes later he tried again, and when he knocked off the bar a second time he knew that he was in real trouble. Only one more chance remained and if he missed again he would be out of it altogether. He could not understand why he was hitting the bar at a height that he ordinarily cleared with great ease. In a cold sweat Bob made his third and final jump, and just got over the bar. Then, oddly enough, a few minutes later, when it was raised six inches higher, he sailed over it on the first jump without any trouble at all. After getting through that first agonizing round, the final seemed easy to him. He repeated his 1952 success and again set an Olympic record, this time at 14 feet 11½ inches.

More and more records went by the wayside, including the supposedly unattainable standard set by Bob Mathias. The new Olympic record-maker in the decathlon was Milton Campbell, who had finished second to Mathias at Helsinki. At Melbourne the new champion ran up a total of 7,937 points, just 50 more than Bob had scored four years earlier.

Perhaps the most popular victory of the Games was the one that went to Alain Mimoun, who had been runner-up to Zatopek three times in Olympic competition — at 10,000 meters in London, at 5,000 and 10,000 meters in Helsinki. The mustachioed Algerian was trying the marathon for the first time even though he knew that his old rival Zatopek was going to be in the race. In defiance of superstition, Mimoun wore the number 13 on his track suit. Just before the race began he learned that he had become a father and perhaps it was the good news that put the needed stamina in his body.

At any rate, it turned out to be Mimoun's day. After trailing the first half of the race, the swarthy Algerian put on the pressure, took the lead, and came home a solitary winner in the time of 2 hours 25 seconds.

The capacity crowd of 103,000 in the stadium cheered him wildly as he broke the tape, but the aging Zatopek, who trotted in a few minutes later to finish sixth, got just as big an ovation. And for once the Czech seemed to be running as if he enjoyed it. He was sincerely pleased that his old rival had at last won a gold medal.

The United States was represented by its best all-around men's track and field team since the Olympics began. The Americans dominated as never before, achieving a 48-year peak of 15 firsts out of 24 events. Russia was runner-up with three victories, and no other nation won more than one gold medal.

In the women's track and field it was a different story. The Australian girls took four of the nine events listed, the Russians two, and the United States, Poland, and Czechoslovakia one each. The sole Yankee victor was Mildred McDaniel who cleared 5 feet 9¼ inches in the high jump for an Olympic record.

Australia produced the fastest female ever seen on the cinder paths. She was Betty Cuthbert, who was winner of the 100-meter and 200-meter sprints and ran anchor on the victorious 400-meter relay team. While winning her three gold medals, Betty shattered or equaled world and Olympic records in each race.

Andrea Mead Lawrence of Rutland, Vermont, won the slalom and the giant slalom for the United States in the 1952 Olympics at Oslo.

CHAPTER 9

THE WINTER GAMES

WINTER SPORTS had a slow and uncertain beginning in the modern Olympic era. Not until 1908, when the Games had been in existence for a dozen years, did the first winter sport appear on the Olympic lists. That year at London, as part of the summer Games, figure skating was added to the program and four competitions were held — for men, for women, doubles (pair skating), and an event listed as "special figures" which was never again put into competition.

The new sport of figure skating did not create much spectator enthusiasm and it was dropped from the Olympics for 12 years. When it was revived, at Antwerp in 1920, a second winter sport, ice hockey, was also listed.

Following the Antwerp Games, the International Olympic Committee was flooded with the demands of skiing and speed skating enthusiasts for a larger and more varied program of winter sports. The I.O.C. was cool to the idea at first on the ground that the Olympics were traditionally summer games ever since the ancient Greeks first held them, and they should remain so. However, the clamor for more winter sports grew so loud, especially by European enthusiasts, that the I.O.C. finally yielded and agreed to stage a separate set of Games in the winter of 1924. They were held in Chamonix, France, more or less as an experiment, but they were so successful that the I.O.C. announced that they would be conducted thereafter every four years, in the same calendar year as the summer Olympics.

At Chamonix, in addition to the ice hockey and figure skating contests previously held, there were competitions in skiing, speed skating, and bobsledding, and demonstrations in curling and the military ski race and shoot. In the five competitive sports there were a total of 16 events and of these the United States captured only one — the 500-meter skating race, which was won by Charles Jewtraw. As expected, the Norwegians and Finns ran away with just about every event that required skis or skates, and Canada won the ice hockey for the second time.

Norway produced a triple winner in the peerless racer, Clas Thunberg, victor in the 1,500 meters, 5000 meters and the all-around speed skating event. The tireless Thunberg was good at any distance on the ice. He placed second in the long 10,000-meter race and tied for third in the 500-meter sprint, thus winning medals in all five of the skating races.

Norway produced another competitor who caused a stir among the spectators, but not because of any medals won. It was the age and size of the performer that stirred the crowds. She was a tiny blond, doll-like creature only 10 years old named Sonja Henie, and she was in the women's figure skating event. The incredible child had won the championship of Norway a few weeks before, defeating a field of mature and experienced women. Her parents had entered her in the winter Olympics for the experience — and that was just what she got. Sonja finished in last place, but at least she knew what it was like to compete against the greatest skating stars in the world.

The girl was not discouraged by her showing. In fact, she was rather glad that she had not won any honors. "I don't like to think what might have happened if I had become Olympic champion at the age of 10," she wrote in her autobiography, ("Wings on My Feet" Prentice-Hall, N.Y., 1940). "It might have gone to my head, and surely would have robbed me of the fun and fine training of four years' work toward that goal."

Indeed Sonja did work toward the Olympic goal in the next four years, at ballet lessons as well as figure skating. She was fortunate in having a father who was a sports fan and a successful businessman, and could afford to give her the best instruction available.

The little blue-eyed blonde continued to amaze all who saw her perform on the ice. Between Olympics she won the Norwegian women's championship four more times and in 1927, when the world tournament was held in her home town of Oslo, she entered it — and won! It was hard to believe that this girl of 13 was the champion of the world.

Sonja was on the threshold of a career that was to last for more than a quarter of a century and bring her world-wide fame and fortune as an ice-show queen and movie star. But the finest moment she ever had was at Oslo when the judges announced that she had won and she was brought to the royal box and presented to King Haakon and Queen Maude of Norway.

The second Olympic winter Games were held in St. Moritz, Switzerland, in 1928, and again it was the Scandinavians who dominated the skiing, speed skating, and figure skating events. The Americans, however, won the two bobsled races.

Sonja, a veteran campaigner at the age of 14, whirled, glided, and spun to her first Olympic victory and had the crowds gasping. Veteran or not, she had enough of the little girl in her to break down and weep in the locker room after she knew that she had won.

How was it possible for a mere girl to triumph over the best women figure skaters in the world? In her autobiography Sonja says that until the 1928 winter Games "figure skating had been rather stiff and pedantic in form" but that she dared to try something new — a blend of ballet and skating — and it won the judges' approval.

Part of a skater's performance is composed of the compulsory "school figures," which are standardized and rigid in form, and must be executed with the utmost precision. They count 60% in the score. The other part, however, is "free skating" (worth 40%), and in this phase the contestant is given more freedom and can try jumps and spins of his own invention.

"I am sure that my introduction of dance pattern into my free skating program had a great deal to do with my winning the 1928 championship," she says in her book. "As a matter of history, good skaters in all countries since then have come to build their free skating programs to a large extent on dance choreography."

Sonja's imaginative skating pleased the crowds as well as the judges. America saw her for the first time in 1929 when she gave an exhibition in Madison Square Garden in New York and was an instant success. Capacity crowds of 15,000 jammed the Garden nightly to see the 16-year-old "Norwegian Doll" cavort about on the ice in dazzling costumes. That winter she toured the United States and Canada and skated before packed arenas in almost every city.

Sonja paid her second visit to America in 1932, this time to defend her Olympic championship at Lake Placid, New York, where the third winter Games were held. Again she won, and again the Scandinavian nations showed their vast superiority in all four of the skiing events — the 18- and 50-kilometer cross-country races, the combined cross-country and jump, and the jump. As usual, the Yankees won the bobsled races and Canada the hockey.

Unusual, though, was America's sweep of the four speed skating events. There were two double winners — Jack Shea, victor in the 500-meter and 1,500-meter races, and Irving Jaffee who took the 5,000 meters and the 10,000 meters. The reason for the unprecedented American triumphs was the unfamiliarity of the European athletes with the American speed racing rules, which were used for the first time in the Olympics.

Sonja Henie, the Norwegian Doll, as she looked at the 1932 Olympics at Lake Placid, New York. She was then 18 years old, a world and Olympic figure skating champion. *Right,* Gretchen Fraser, America's first Olympic skiing champion. She won the slalom at St. Moritz in 1948.

Under the European rules the entries race in pairs against the clock with honors going to the man who makes the fastest time. Each man races only once.

In the American system the contestants race against each other as in foot racing. Trial heats are held to cut down the field and regardless of the times recorded in those heats, the man who wins the final wins the event. This system requires something more than mere speed. A racer must know how to pace himself, how to avoid getting boxed in, and how to jockey for position on the turns. He must be aware of his opponents at all times, for he is, after all, racing against them, not the clock.

The Europeans had never before raced on the ice under American rules and they were at a disadvantage. Before the races began they protested vigorously, but it did no good. The American rules prevailed, much to their expressed dissatisfaction.

As before, the Americans made a dismal showing in all of the skiing events. This was perhaps understandable in view of the fact that their European opponents were the result of many generations of development, whereas the sport was relatively new in the United States.

The Lake Placid Olympics, however, gave great impetus to the sport in America. Thousands of people who had never seen skiing before were fascinated by the way the European Olympians flashed down the slopes on their wooden wings. In 1933, the year after the winter Olympics, the first ski tow was installed at Woodstock, Vermont, and this was the beginning of a ski boom that soon swept the country. At that time there were no more than a handful of skiers in the United States. Today, thanks in great part to the Olympics, an estimated 3,000,000 skiers take to the hills every winter.

The boom, however, did not produce any American ski champions at Garmisch-Partenkirchen, in the Bavarian Alps in Germany, where the fourth winter Olympics were held in 1936.

The speed racing was conducted under European rules and the Norwegians made a sweep of the four events, three of them going to Ivar Ballangrud, who won the 500, the 5,000 and the 10,000 meters, and got second in the 1,500 meters.

The Norwegian Doll, now fully grown at the age of 22, but as petite and lovely as ever — she weighed about 100 pounds and was five feet tall — won her third straight Olympic figure skating championship, a feat that has never been duplicated by a woman.[1] Shortly afterwards she turned professional and began a new and fabulous career.

As the queen of her own gorgeously costumed ice show, she toured the country and was a sensational hit wherever she played. Sonja originated the ice show and popularized the long-ignored art of figure skating. She made a fortune from her shows and became the first girl athlete to earn a million dollars.

The Olympic fire was cold for a dozen years, until 1948, when a renewal of the winter Games was held at St. Moritz, France. With a total of 878 competitors representing 28 nations, the fifth winter Olympics were the biggest yet, and from an American standpoint the best.

For the first time in the history of the winter Games, the United States won gold medals in skiing and in figure skating.

Mrs. Gretchen Fraser, a pretty pig-tailed young woman from Vancouver, Washington, broke America's ski jinx by winning the slalom.[2] Then Dick Button, a sprightly 18-year-old Harvard freshman from Englewood, New Jersey, took top honors in figure skating.

The news of the two victories was received with cheers in the United States, even though most of the medals in the Games went, as usual, to the European athletes. America had made a reasonably good showing and at last had won championships in events that always before had been beyond reach. Still, there was a wide gap between the American and European men skiers. In the history of the Olympics the best the United States had ever done was 10th in the downhill.[3]

In the next winter Games, held at Oslo in 1952, America's male skiers showed improvement with a fifth in the downhill and a sixth in

[1] Gillis Grafstrom of Sweden won the men's Olympic figure skating championship three times — in 1920, 1924, and 1928.

[2] The slalom, which was introduced in the 1948 winter Games, is a downhill race against time through a number of pairs of flags on poles (called "gates"). They are placed so that the course winds and twists in zigzag fashion. The slalom is a test of the most highly developed precision in the technique of skiing.

[3] The downhill, also introduced in 1948, differs from the slalom in that the course is longer and steeper, and the racer is restricted only to the general boundaries of the course, plus occasional control gates. Like the slalom, it is a race against time, only one skier competing at a time.

the giant slalom, which is longer than the regular slalom and has more gates. That was nothing, though, compared to the performance turned in by Mrs. Andrea Mead Lawrence, a 19-year-old wizard on skis.

Andy Mead, as she is known to her friends, sped to victory in the giant slalom on the first day of the Games to send the United States off to a roaring start. The tall, 5-foot 7-inch housewife from Rutland, Vermont, swept down the hazardous 640-yard descent in 2 minutes 6.8 seconds and fell into the arms of her husband, Dave Lawrence, a Dartmouth graduate and Olympic skier. Andy had outclassed a field of 44 feminine skiers from 15 countries.

A couple of days later she tried the downhill, but here luck was against her. She took two hard spills and finished 17th. Such bone-jarring tumbles might shatter the nerve of the ordinary competitor, but the slim-hipped, 130-pound Andy could not wait to get at her next event, the slalom.

Halfway down, in her first run, a ski tip caught one of the gates and down went Andy. Quickly she bounced up and sped on her way, but the spill had cost her at least three precious seconds. (In the slalom two heats are run by each contestant and the total time of the heats determines the final standings.) When the first-heat results were announced, Andy was in fourth place and she knew that she would have to go all out in the second heat to make up for her slow time in the first.

She started off with a poled jump and fairly flew down the course. With reckless speed she cut corners and twisted and zipped through the gates. The cheering crowd sensed that she was making the fastest time of anyone, but would it be fast enough to win? Andy's time in the second heat was 1 minute 3.4 seconds, a full two seconds faster than any woman had been able to do all day. And it was fast enough to win for her — but with the narrow margin of $8/10$ths of a second over Ossi Reichert of Germany. Despite her first-heat header, Andy had become the first American skier ever to win two Olympic gold medals.

The United States won two more gold medals for the finest record ever compiled by an American team in Europe. Dick Button annexed his second straight Olympic title with one of his inimitable performances, and Ken Henry of Chicago flashed the best time in the 500-meter skating race to win in 43.2 seconds.

It was a Norwegian, though, who dominated the speed skating and became the hero of his country. He was Hjalmar Andersen, a 28-year-old truck driver, who won races at 5,000 meters, 1,500 meters, and 10,000 meters on consecutive days and broke two Olympic records and one world record.

The sturdy Norwegians stood above the 30 nations at Oslo when the final results were tallied. In addition to Andersen's triple victories, they won four skiing events for a total of seven gold medals. America was next best in the number of victories.

The United States did not have as much to cheer about at the 1956 winter Games, which were held at Cortina, a mountain town in Italy. Only two gold medals out of a possible 24 were won by Americans and both were in the figure skating singles. Tenley Albright, a wisp of a girl from Newton Center, Massachusetts, won the women's event and Hayes Alan Jenkins of Colorado took the men's.

Tenley's victory was a popular one, for she had suffered some bad luck during her career. She was runner-up in the 1952 Olympics at the age of 16 and the following year she won the world championship at Davos, Switzerland. Then in 1954, in the Bislet Olympic Stadium in Oslo, Norway, where she appeared to defend her world title, the blond Tenley committed the cardinal sin of figure skating. She fell, and it wasn't just a little slip. She sat down squarely on the ice. The crowd sat stunned as she regained her feet and continued her routine, but the damage had been done.

A fall by a champion figure skater is something like a star slugger striking out with the bases loaded in a World Series game, or a champion golfer whiffing a ball in a national tournament. It is never supposed to happen, and it is most humiliating when it does.

After she had finished her performance and before the result was announced, Tenley was in a corner of the rink practicing the double-loop jump that had caused her fall. Soon came the announcement that she had lost her world crown to Gundi Busch of Germany.

Next year Tenley went to Vienna and with a performance that was as near to perfection as possible regained the championship of the world. She was the first woman ever to lose that title and then get it back again.

In Cortina, before the Games began, the blond beauty was severely cut in practice and her coach feared that she would be unable

Dick Button, Olympic figure skating champion in 1948 and 1952 is welcomed home by an admiring group of neighborhood kids in Englewood, New Jersey.

to perform. However, her father, a prominent Boston surgeon, flew from the United States and took care of her so that she could appear in the Olympics.

Most of the honors at Cortina went to the Russians, who made their winter debut with a large team of men and women athletes and took six gold medals out of a possible 24. One of them — and here was a surprise — was for winning the hockey crown, which up to then had been the exclusive property of Canada except once — in 1936 when Great Britain won it. The Soviets took three of the four speed skating races and two women's skiing events.

The star of the Games, however, was an Austrian, a handsome dark-haired 21-year-old plumber named Tony Sailer, who won three skiing events — the giant slalom, the regular slalom, and the downhill. The Austrian perfectionist stole the spotlight not only because of his triple win but by the way he won. His form was so flawless and his time so fast that no one was within sight of him in any of the three

Tenley Albright of Newton, Mass. won the figure skating championship at Cortina, Italy in 1956. Here she performs before the judges with her free skating routine.

races. Thanks to Sailer, Austria made the next best showing after Russia with four gold medals, one of which was in the figure skating pairs. Next came Switzerland and Finland, each with three first places, and then came the two gold medal nations — Sweden, Norway, and the United States.

Despite America's mediocre record, the 1956 Games were well conducted and were the largest in winter history in number of competitors, 923, in nations represented, 32, and in events listed, 24.

When the I.O.C. announced that the 1960 winter Games would be held in Squaw Valley, California, there was considerable criticism of the choice in Olympic circles, especially among European officials and athletes. Why such a far-off place, they wanted to know. It was more than 3,000 miles from New York, twice that distance from most European countries, and the nearest city to it was Reno, 40 miles away with a population of only 35,000. How could such a remote place attract crowds, and what did the new and untested winter resort have in the way of Olympic facilities and accommodations?

What Squaw Valley had, after four years of preparation and some $15,000,000 poured into it by the federal government and the states of California and Nevada, were these facilities: a $3,500,000 ice arena for hockey and figure skating with 8,500 seats, a 400-meter speed skating oval, several ski courses for the Alpine events (slalom, giant slalom and downhill) and cross-country races, six ski lifts, three ski jumps, an Olympic village, inns, restaurants, shops, and a parking area for 12,000 cars.

Squaw Valley also had Walt Disney as head of the pageantry committee to lend a Hollywood touch to the opening day ceremonies on February 18. Taking part in them were bands and choirs from 52 high schools comprising 3,800 students and 2,000 white "doves of peace," which were released from a battery of cakes. Vice President Richard Nixon declared the Games formally open, and Carol Heiss, America's star figure skater from Ozone Park, New York, recited the Olympic oath on behalf of the athletes:

"We swear that we will take part in these Olympic Games in the true spirit of sportsmanship, and that we will respect and abide by the rules that govern them, for the glory of sport and the honor of our country."

The ceremonies ended with the rocketing of parachute-borne national flags and the release of thousands of balloons while the athletes marched out of the arena. There were 740 contestants at Squaw Valley and 30 nations were represented — a slight decrease from the previous winter Games. However, a new high was reached in the number of events listed. There were 27 on the program, three more than ever before because of the addition of women's speed skating races and a strange new event called the biathlon.[4]

[4] A combination of cross-country skiing and shooting, the biathlon is raced on a course of 20 kilometers, which is about 12 miles. Along the way the racers, who carry rifles, stop at four firing stations to shoot five rounds at targets at distances of 100, 150, 200, and 250 meters. Two minutes are added to a contestant's time for each miss and the man who finishes in the fastest net time is the winner. Although the biathlon is new to the Olympics, it is an old event, going back to 1767 as part of the first ski meet in history — at Oslo, Norway. It was included in the winter Games at the strong request of the Russians and Scandinavians, who value the sport for its military as well as sporting features.

Because of the Russians' success at Cortina and their intensive all-year-sports program to develop Olympic athletes, they were expected to take almost half of the 27 gold medals. They did not prove to be that strong, however. True, they did win the most — seven, one of which was shared with Norway because of a tie in the men's 1,500-meter speed skating race. But if it had not been for the speed skating events (there were eight on the program and European rules were used), they would have won only one gold medal. And the Soviet men could give thanks to their womenfolk because the ladies won four of the seven gold medals, three in speed skating and one in the 10-kilometer cross-country ski race. This was Russia's only victory off the ice.

The pre-Olympic form chart was off elsewhere, too. High hopes were held for America's girl skiers Betsy Snite from Norwich, Vermont, and Penny Pitou, a 21-year-old pony-tailed blond from Guilford, New Hampshire. The New England girls had grown up on skis and between Olympics had trained long and hard. The winter before the 1960 Games they toured Europe and between them won several Alpine events in international competition against Europe's best. Of the two Penny had the better record and was given an excellent chance to win gold medals in the slalom and downhill. In Europe she had consistently defeated the same women she was going to race against in Squaw Valley.

Luck, however, was not with the American girls. In the downhill race Penny started off first and streaked down the top part of the mountain at a speed estimated at 60 miles per hour. For three quarters of the blazing trip she was in perfect control, but then at the end of the steepest *schuss* (a straight downhill run) she came to a 90° left turn in the course dubbed the "Airplane Turn." As she flew into it like a plane banking into an airport, she hit a bump, staggered, slowed up, and almost fell. Only will power kept her from going down, but the Airplane Turn had cost her at least two seconds.

Later, when Betsy Snite roared into it, she fell badly and lost her right ski. She was out of the race completely and was brought down the course well shaken up. At least a dozen girls took headers at the fatal turn, including two other Americans.

One contender who managed to keep her feet all the way was Heidi Biebl, a 19-year-old factory worker from West Germany. In perfect control, Heidi sacrificed some speed by starting her turn on the

Opening ceremonies in the new ice arena at Squaw Valley, California, for the 1960 winter Games.

schuss before reaching the trouble point. Showing extremely fine balance, she banked nicely on the Airplane Turn and came down the final pitch to the finish line in the familiar crouch racers use to cut down wind resistance. Her final time of 1 minute 37.6 seconds for the 5,997-foot plunge was the fastest, exactly a second better than Penny made to get second place. The surprise winner had been beaten by Penny several times in Europe.

Penny and Betsy got their second chance a few days later in the giant slalom, a course nearly a mile long with 57 staggered gates. In this race the gates are much farther apart than in the special slalom, and, therefore, a skier can step on the throttle without much danger of being caught going too fast on the turns — a hazard that exists in the special. Penny went down wide open and catapulted through all the gates without wavering, but her time was not quite fast enough to win. Again she was defeated by a surprise winner, a chunky little French girl named Yvonne Ruegg, who beat her by the hairline margin of $\frac{1}{10}$th of a second. Betsy Snite was fourth. It was a bitter disappointment for Penny to have missed the gold medal for the second time.

One more chance remained for the American girls, in the slalom, which was run on two courses, each with 53 gates. The 43 contestants ran their first heat on one course, then switched to the other for their second. After the first run Betsy was in fourth place and Penny was close behind her. The second run would tell the story — and it was a sad one for Penny. She crashed near the top of the course, then arose but finished slowly, knowing that she was out of contention. Betsy, though, came down flying all the way, and her time of 55.5 seconds was the fastest but it was not enough to win. In the over-all time Anne Heggtveit of Canada recorded 1 minute 49.6 seconds for first place and Betsy was more than two seconds behind her. With her defeat went one of the United States' greatest opportunities to score a sweep of the women's Alpine competition since the winter Games began. In the three Alpine events, Americans were favored, but in all three they finished second.

As if to make up for it, the United States hockey team brought unexpected joy to the spectators at Squaw Valley and to the millions of Americans who for the first time viewed the winter Olympics on television.

The American team, which included a soldier, a fireman, two carpenters, and two insurance agents, was not given an outside chance before the tournament began. The experts picked Russia and Canada to reach the final round and battle it out for the championship.

Unnoticed and unsung were the American hockeymen, even after they had won their first four games and had defeated Czechoslovakia, Australia, Sweden, and Germany. Next on the list was Canada, a team that had scored 40 goals while giving up only three. Few thought that the Americans could get by the Canadians — they had never done so in 40 years of Olympic competition — but the impossible happened. Canada went down to defeat, 2 to 1, in a thriller — and now there was Russia, undefeated but tied once by the Swedes. This was the big one for the Americans. If they could get by Russia, they would be in the final round. The contest took place on February 27, a Saturday, on the ninth day of the Games.

The game was under way only a couple of minutes when Bill Cleary scored for America on a pass from his brother Bob, an insurance agent from Westwood, Massachusetts. But within five minutes Russia scored twice to lead, 2 to 1. Between periods in the locker room Coach Jack Riley told the team, "Everyone in the nation is counting on you guys. There are millions watching you on television."

In the second period the Americans scored again on a brother-to-brother pass, only this time it was another pair of brothers. Bill Christian, one of the carpenters, took a pass from his brother, Roger, the other carpenter, and the score was tied. In the third period Bill Christian shot home another goal to give the United States a 3-2 lead, and that was the score when the game ended.

The next day the amazing Americans clashed with the Czechs in the championship round. Trailing 4-3 after two periods, the Americans got a surprise visit in their dressing room from Nik Sologubov, captain of the Russian team, who urged the players to take a whiff of oxygen as a pickup before the final period. Sologubov did not speak a word of English but he got the message across in sign language. Most of the players accepted Sologubov's suggestion.

Then they went out on the ice and whether it was the oxygen or determination and courage will never be known, but they played like fiends and overwhelmed the Czechs with a six-goal rally. In one 67-second span they scored three goals. The final score was 9-4, for America's first hockey gold medal since the game was introduced into the Olympics in 1920.

The jubilant coach, Jack Riley, said afterward that while the oxygen may have helped in the elevation of over 6,000 feet, "I think the lift was mostly psychological," and pointed out that Bill Cleary, who made one goal and assisted for three more in the final period, did not take a sniff.

The United States won a total of three gold medals at Squaw Valley, all of them on the ice. The first one was not gained until the Games were five days old, when Carol Heiss skated to victory before the foot-stomping applause of 8,500 chilled spectators in the arena.

All other Olympic events are run off in seconds, minutes, at most an hour or two (for the long cross-country races), but figure skating is a four-day war of nerves. For three days the field of 26 girls from 13 nations had executed the compulsory school figures but everything hung on the last day's performance of free skating.

Each exhibition took five minutes, ticked off by an electric clock. When Carol finished, the nine judges credited her with top-heavy scores. Six points is perfection but the judges rarely give anyone that many. Carol came close, though. Two officials gave her 5.9, three scored her at 5.8, and no one gave her less than 5.5.

When the blond 20-year-old New York University student left the ice, she was nearly mobbed by excited spectators. They knew that she had won even though all the results were not yet in. Her total score of 1,490.1 points easily topped the field.

In 1956, at Cortina, Carol had finished second to Tenley Albright by the almost invisible and heartbreaking margin of 1.5 points. But a few weeks later she beat Tenley in the world championships to become at 16 the youngest titleholder since Sonja Henie won the crown in 1927. From there she went on to win three more world championships consecutively before her ultimate triumph in the Olympics.

A few years before, Carol had promised her mother that she would not turn professional until she had won an Olympic gold medal. Mrs. Heiss died of cancer in 1956 but Carol never forgot her promise and fulfilled it at Squaw Valley.

After her mother's death, Carol took over the running of the family home, a modest stucco house. Her German-born father, Edward, who is a baker, followed his daughter's Olympic victory by television in the family home.

America's other gold medalist was David Jenkins, whose brother, Hayes, had won the figure-skating championship at Cortina. David, a slim medical student at Western Reserve University, kept the title in the family with an almost flawless performance on the final day of the competition. He had to come from behind to do it, too.

He trailed Karol Divin of Czechoslovakia in the compulsory school figures at the end of the third day but he had in store a daring assortment of routines for the free skating. Even Divin conceded that Jenkins would outscore him in the closing program, for the American was known to excel in free skating.

David lived up to expectations and when he finished his spec-

Carol Heiss (center) was America's first gold medalist at Squaw Valley. Here the champion figure skater is flanked by runner-up Sjoukje Dijkstra (left) of Holland and Barbara Roles, of the United States, third.

tacular routines the judges gave him the highest marks ever awarded in the Olympics for his almost flawless performance. Only one official rated him as low as 5.8. Seven gave him 5.9 points, and the remaining one awarded him the perfect mark of 6, a figure that is considered to be virtually unattainable.

Shortly after the Olympics, Carol Heiss went to Vancouver, British Columbia, and gained her fifth world championship. Then she came home and after receiving a hero's welcome in New York City made two important announcements — first, that she was going to marry Hayes Alan Jenkins, the 1956 Olympic champion and winner of four world titles, and since his retirement from figure skating, a lawyer in Akron, Ohio; second, that she planned a professional career but would move to Akron following her marriage and would complete her college education in Ohio.

Thanks to its hockey team and two figure skaters, the United States finished in a triple tie for third place with Sweden and Norway in the number of gold medals won. Finland, Canada, and Switzerland each gained two, and France and Austria one apiece. Russia, as noted before, ended with seven, followed by Germany with four.[5]

The 11-day long Games were held in near-perfect weather, but attendance did not come up to expectations. A total of about 240,000 people witnessed the contests, although 385,000 were expected. Still, it surpassed the attendance of all previous winter Games except the 500,000 aggregate at Oslo in 1952.

More important than attendance or number of gold medals won was the widespread comradeship of the athletes. Even the Russians, who always before had been tight-lipped and aloof, warmed up and became more friendly. There was not a single unpleasant incident during the entire Games.

Bill Henry, the radio director at Squaw Valley, expressed the feelings of everyone who took part in the Games when he said at the closing ceremonies:

"The competition has been great. Championships have been decided by inches and fractions of seconds. Sportsmanship was never more universally demonstrated."

The assembled athletes who heard him had marched in, not in national groups as they had at the opening ceremonies, but as one unit without any separation of national contingents. The friendly, smiling athletes, many with arms interlocked, symbolized the Olympic theory that competition is among individuals rather than nations, which, after all, is the idea that Baron de Coubertin had in the first place.

[5] This adds up to 28, whereas there were only 27 events. Because of the tie between Norway and Russia in the 5,000-meters speed skating race, both nations were credited with a first place, and second place was not given to any country.

CHAPTER 10

ROME, 1960

THE GAMES WENT TO ROME in the summer of 1960 and the Eternal City witnessed the biggest and grandest show since gladiators fought to the death in the ancient Colosseum and chariots whirled around the Circus Maximus. Rome outdid itself to make the Games glorious, perhaps to make amends for its "crime" of sixteen centuries ago when Emperor Theodosius I of Rome decreed the end of the Olympics after they had run for more than a thousand years.

For four years Italy prepared for the Games. The nation had always been poorly equipped athletically but the Italians more than made up for it with a huge sports construction program that cost some $50,000,000. The money came from the government's share of a weekly gambling pool on soccer. The windfall enabled the Italian Olympic Committee to erect new stadiums, sports palaces, arenas, and playing fields such as the Games had never seen before. The result was a superb blend of the ancient and modern worlds.

In the mossy Basilica of Maxentius, a public assembly hall built in the third century, wrestlers grappled for Olympic medals. Lithe gymnasts swung and spun in the Baths of Caracalla, where wealthy Romans took steam baths more than 1,500 years ago. The marathon started at the Capitol and part of it was run on the Appian Way, a military road that once felt the tread of Caesar's legions.

In contrast were the modern structures, the greatest of which was the Olympic Stadium with a spectator capacity of 100,000 and

Decathlon champion Rafer Johnson carries the American flag as the United States Olympic team of three hundred athletes parades at the opening ceremonies in Rome, August 25, 1960.

underground dressing rooms for 1,500 athletes. It was the site of all track and field finals, the focal point of the Games. Nearby was the Swimming Stadium (there were seven pools in all), the Marble Stadium for field hockey, the Flaminio Stadium (soccer) and the Little Sports Palace (weightlifting). In another part of the city was the Big Sports Palace (basketball and boxing) and close by stood the Palace of Congresses (fencing) and the Velodrome, a curved wooden track for bicycle racing with grandstand seats for 20,000. In all, there were 13 stadiums with a total seating capacity of 300,000. To the Games came a record number of athletes (5,902) representing 84 nations — also a new high — to compete in 150 events in the 18 sports on the program.

In men's track and field, the blue-ribbon Olympic sport, the United States seemed supreme — at least on the form chart. In the opinion of most experts it was the strongest team in track history. Among those who figured to be certain gold medal winners were:

110

John Thomas, a 19-year-old Negro of Boston University who had cleared the once-impossible 7-foot barrier in the high jump 37 times and had soared to a record 7 feet, 3¾ inches. No one had ever caused him to extend himself.

Ray Norton, 23, a statuesque Negro who had been unbeatable in the sprints for two years and had been clocked in world record time in the 100 and 200 meters. "In a class by himself," said United States Olympic track coach, Larry Snyder, of the consistent Norton.

Harold Connolly, 28-year-old veteran, gold medal winner in the hammer throw at Melbourne in 1956, and holder of the world record of 225 feet, 4 inches.

Ralph Boston, a 25-year-old Negro who made track history two weeks before the Rome Games by breaking Jesse Owens' world mark in the broad jump with a leap of 26 feet, 11¼ inches. (Owens' record, 26′ 8¼″, set at Ann Arbor, Michigan in 1935, was the oldest one on the books. "Another old friend gone," smiled Jesse when he was told that his last remaining record had fallen.)

Don (Tarzan) Bragg, a stocky 200-pound pole vaulter with a wrestler's build, who had sailed higher (15 feet, 9½ inches) than any man.

Rafer Johnson, 25, a 6-foot, 3-inch Negro giant from California who had scored the greatest number of points in the decathlon (8,683) to break by 326 points the world record of Russia's Vasily Kuznetsov. In the eyes of most track coaches, this feat made him the finest all-around athlete in the world.

There were other champions and record-breakers on the 65-man team that Coach Snyder called "great and dedicated." "We may not match the Melbourne team's gold medals," he said, "but we'll do well again."

How well? Fine, it seemed, as the first day of track and field competition (August 31) got under way. America's Bill Nieder, an Army lieutenant, won the shotput with an Olympic record heave of 64 feet, 6¾ inches to defeat his arch rival, Parry O'Brien, who was trying for his third straight gold medal. Parry made a toss that was better than his winning performances at Helsinki and Melbourne but it was only good for a silver medal at Rome. Third place went to Dallas Long of Phoenix, Arizona, thus giving the United States a clean sweep in the very first track and field event.

Wearing a brace because of a game leg, shotputter Bill Nieder makes an Olympic record toss of 64 feet, 6¾ inches for America's first track and field gold medal.

It was a different story the next day, though, a day that has since been known as Black Thursday. The first stunner was the downfall of highly favored Ray Norton in the 100-meter dash. There were six men in the final and Ray finished a dead last. The winner was Armin Hary, a 22-year-old German who gave his country its first victory in an Olympic sprint. Dave Sime, the hard-luck athlete who had missed the Melbourne Games because of a pulled muscle, was an eyelash behind the German (both were clocked in 10.2) and Peter Radford of Great Britain was third. Actually, there was only a yard and a half between the winner and last place Ray Norton, whose time was 10.4. Still, it was the first time since 1928 that an American had not won this event.

That was the first of the one-two punch America got on Black Thursday. The second, and harder blow, came late in the afternoon when John Thomas, the world's most consistent and most unbeatable high jumper — the surest bet on earth to win a gold medal — went down to defeat.

For the first time in his young life Thomas found himself competing against equals and near-equals and the pressure was just too much for him. When the bar was put at 7 feet, ¼ inch there were four survivors — Thomas and three Russians. Two of the Russians had never before cleared seven feet but this time they did and then when all four got over the bar it was moved up to 7 feet, 1 inch.

Thomas had the disadvantage of jumping last and while waiting his turn he saw two of the Russians clear the new height. He had never seen anyone jump that high before and he began to feel the strain. He was so nervous that his legs trembled. As 70,000 people watched in absolute silence Thomas made his first try. His trailing leg did not clear the bar and he missed badly. Once more he tried and the bar went down again. In his third and final try the bar toppled into the sawdust pit with him and he lay on his back, staring unbelievingly at the sky. Then slowly he got up and walked grief-stricken to the side lines. The invincible one who had set world records indoors and out with a top mark of 7 feet, 3¾ inches, had fluffed his biggest moment and had to settle for third place and a bronze medal. "He is not used to competition," said one of his conquerors. "He is too young."

There was one more blow that day. America's three crack 800-

meter men failed to get by the semi-final round, but the next day Yankee fortunes turned dramatically. In the 400-meter hurdles reliable Glenn Davis, a winner at Melbourne, did it again and helped give the United States a one-two-three sweep in the race.

Ralph Boston lived up to his pre-Olympic form and won with a fine broad jump of 26 feet, 7¾ inches and endeared himself to thousands of American TV watchers when he held his gold medal aloft and in a moment of supreme happiness said, "Mom, if you're looking in, this is for you!"

Wilma Rudolph, a tall, pretty girl from Tennessee State, which is Ralph Boston's Alma Mater, bolstered America's hopes when she walked away from the field in the 100-meter dash. She broke the world record (11 seconds flat) by three tenths of a second but it was disallowed because of a light tail wind.

Americans were cheered by the comeback but there was another black day in store for them — Black Saturday, September 3. On that day the United States eight-oared crew from the Naval Academy finished a sorry fifth behind Germany, Canada, Czechoslovakia, and France in that order, thus ending a victory streak dating back to 1920.

As before, the United States took a double blow in track and field when two ace performers failed to come through. Harold Connolly, the hammer-throwing world champion, and ten feet better than any other man on earth, not only did not win the hammer throw but did not even qualify for the final round. "I couldn't get the iron ball out. I just didn't have it," said the disappointed and bewildered Connolly.

And in the 200-meter dash, which American sprinters had won ten times in twelve Olympics, Ray Norton, again the heavy favorite, again finished last in the six-man final. A little-known Italian named Livio Berruti broke the tape just in front of America's Les Carney. The United States, which had won both dashes in the previous five Olympics (back beyond Jesse Owens' day), now had lost both. "I just don't know what's wrong," said downhearted Ray Norton. When he was told that he had left his spiked shoes at the track, he said, "I don't want to see them ever again." Ray was to see them again, though — in the 400-meter relay, where worse luck than ever was in store for him.

Chris Von Saltza, sixteen-year-old Californian, who won three swimming gold medals, was never without her lucky toy frog.

These two photos taken from a film strip show the disputed finish of the 100-meter swim. Lance Larson, the American, is in Lane 4 and John Devitt of Australia is in Lane 3. Larson, who is under water, appears to touch home just as Devitt (on the surface) starts his last stroke. But the judges did not see it that way and declared Devitt the winner.

Perhaps Ray didn't feel so badly as Wim Essajas, an 800-meter runner who was the one-man team from Surinam (Dutch Guiana) in South America. Wim was not told that the scheduled time of his event, the 800-meter qualifying race, had been changed from afternoon to morning. He awoke at Olympic Village, had a light breakfast, and wandered over to the athletes' lounge to watch television. To his horror, he saw that his race was about to be run. It was too late to get to the Stadium so Wim simply sat down and saw the race on TV. He had come halfway around the world for this frustration that will probably be with him the rest of his life.

Black Saturday was not a total flop for America, however. The week-long swimming meet ended on that day and the Yankee men and women did very well, indeed. They more than made amends for the dismal performance at Melbourne in 1956, when the United States won only five gold medals. This time they won eleven against five for the Australians, their chief rivals. The Yankee girls walloped the Australian girls five events to one, thanks in great part to Chris von Saltza, a sixteen-year-old blonde from California.

In her first race, the 100-meter free style, Chris finished second to Dawn Fraser, a veteran campaigner from Australia. Three days later the two girls met again, this time in the 400-meter free style. Dawn had boasted that she was going to beat Chris again and this may have spurred the American girl on to a supreme effort, which her race certainly was. Chris left Dawn floundering back in fifth place and shattered the Olympic record by three full seconds. Then Chris anchored two relay teams to two world-record victories for a total of three gold medals for herself.

An unpleasant thing happened during the swimming meet that brought no credit to Olympic officialdom. In the men's 100-meter free-style swim, John Devitt of Australia and Lance Larson of the United States were engaged in a terrific duel for the lead over the last 25 meters. It was either man's race as they neared the finish, and they touched home at the same instant — or almost the same instant. Who had won? To most sideline observers, including sports reporters, it seemed that Larson had touched home inches ahead of Devitt. In the pool Larson thought he'd won and Devitt agreed with him. The Australian swam over to Larson and congratulated him. Everyone told Larson he'd won — everyone but the three judges, who went into a long powwow and emerged with the announcement that Larson had not won, but Devitt had. Larson was second, they said. Screams of anguish came from an American Olympic official, Max Ritter, following the announcement. He accused the judges of trickery. To make things more confusing, the official times of the two swimmers as registered by the automatic timers were announced. For Devitt all three registered 55.2 seconds. For Larson all three got him in *faster* time than Devitt had made — in 55 flat, 55.1, and 55.1. How could a man make better time than the winner and not be awarded the victory? Very simple, decided the judges. They changed Larson's time to 55.2, thus ignoring the automatic timers. The Americans were livid at this and made a formal protest but nothing ever came of it.

In track and field things began looking up for the United States once more. Lee Calhoun, the dependable hurdler who had won at Melbourne, flashed home in front for his second Olympic championship in the 110-meter high hurdles and led two fellow-Americans in a one-two-three sweep. Behind them in fourth place was the much-feared German, Martin Lauer, holder of the world record for the distance.

Then came a race that ended in the most dramatic finish in the Olympics. It was the 400 meters, which is really a long sprint and one of the most exhausting of all races. The chief contenders were Otis Davis, a 28-year-old California Negro, and Germany's Carl Kaufmann, a fast and strong quarter miler. Kaufmann took an early lead but Davis, pacing himself well, stayed a few yards behind and floated along. In the turn Davis made his bid and passed the German. Coming into the stretch he had a three-yard lead but the game Kaufmann desperately closed the gap and the two men hit the tape together. Kaufmann in a head-down lunge, broke the tape with his chin; Davis simultaneously broke it with his chest but his body was over the line first, and he won. His time was an astounding 44.9 seconds and a world record.

Another world mark fell that day when Australia's great miler, Herb Elliot, the "wonder runner," crushed all opposition in the 1,500-meter run and won by nearly 30 yards. Elliott, a hawk-faced lean youth of 22, was favored to win the race, for he held the world record for the distance and also for the mile, but no one thought

Yang and Rafer Johnson vie for honors in the 1,500-meter race, last event of the two-day 10-event decathlon. This after dark race was won by Yang but Johnson got the gold medal in the decathlon.

that he would win so easily, or in such fast time. He won in 3 minutes, 35.6 seconds, breaking his own world record by a fraction of a second. His time was the equivalent of a 3:52.6 mile, according to track statisticians who add 17 seconds to a 1,500-meter clocking to get a projected time for the mile, which is about 120 yards longer.

Rafer Johnson, the American decathlon champion, and his friend and rival, C. K. Yang of Taiwan, came down to the last event of the two-day grueling test with only a handful of points separating them. By this time the defending Olympic champion, Vasily Kuznetsov of Russia, was out of the running. In the nine events that had taken place Yang had bettered Johnson in six but the American was so superior in his three specialties — the shotput, discus throw, and javelin throw — that he had more points than Yang when they lined up on the mark in the final event, the 1,500-meter run. Either man could win the gold medal, however. Yang could win it if he bettered Johnson's time by ten seconds. This would make up his narrow deficit in points and put him over the top. Johnson's task was to hang on and not let Yang get too far ahead of him. In previous races at the distance Yang was usually ten seconds faster than Johnson.

From the start Yang took the lead by two steps and ran smoothly, hoping to shake off his rival, but Johnson kept hanging on, plodding doggedly behind Yang and kept pace. On the final turn Yang, summoning his last bit of strength, began to draw away but Johnson never let him get more than five yards ahead and when they finished he was only 1.2 seconds behind. The Chinese youth held his head in dejection, knowing that he had lost a gold medal. Yet he had bettered Johnson in seven of the ten events.

Ray Norton, who finished sixth in both sprints, earned the title as the Games' Most Unfortunate Man for his final performance on the track. Running the second leg in the 400-meter relay, Ray took the baton from starter Frank Budd beyond the limit of the 20-yard passing zone, thus causing the United States to be disqualified. The American team finished first in what would have been a world record (39.4) but Germany, behind by a yard, was awarded first place. Poor Ray later said, "Everything has gone wrong for me. I'm never going to run again. I've had it."

In contrast to Ray's misery was the happiness that came to his Olympic girl friend, Wilma Rudolph. The French called her *La*

The darling of the 1960 Olympics was Wilma Rudolph, America's double dash champion and anchor on the winning 400-meter relay team. Here, the Tennessee girl proudly displays her three gold medals, more than any other American girl ever won in track and field in the Olympics.

Gazelle and she ran like one. After winning the 100-meter sprint she took the 200 meters and then for good measure anchored the women's team to a world record (44.4) in the 400-meter relay. The graceful, popular girl was the only track and field athlete to win three gold medals and the first American woman to win that many in track. Wilma was the darling of the Olympics, not only to her teammates but to all the athletes and the crowds who saw her. She wore her laurels with the poise of a queen. In fact, an English writer spoke of her as having the "carriage a queen should have." A remarkable thing about the fleet-footed girl is that she was crippled by a childhood illness and had to stay in bed for four years, between the ages of four and eight.

The track and field events ended with the marathon, and it was won by a skinny barefooted Ethiopian soldier named Abebe Bikila who had never before run the distance and was considered a rank outsider. No man had ever run a marathon as fast as Abebe (2 hours, 15 minutes and 15.2 seconds) with shoes or without. Because marathon courses vary so much — some may be up and down steep hills, while others may be on fairly level land — a world record is not recognized for this punishing endurance test. Just the same, the little barefooted soldier turned in the fastest time yet.

Although the Games were staged with a monumental splendor unequaled in any other Olympics and the athletes of all nations were friendly and got on well together, the United States felt the impact of the shocking reverses in track and field. Even though the swimmers showed tremendous improvement over 1956 and the boxers exceeded expectations by winning three championships (light middleweight, middleweight, and light heavyweight) and the basketball team was undefeated, there were those stunning defeats in the sprints, the failure to get a man in the final of the 800-meter run, the downfall of the world record holders in the high jump, hammer and javelin throws, and the fifth-place finish of the eight-oared crew.

Even so, the Americans did better than any other nation in men's track and field, winning nine gold medals out of a possible twenty-four. Russia was next best with five, then came Germany, New Zealand, and Poland with two each. After them were the one gold-medal winners: Ethiopia, Italy, Great Britain, and Australia.

Nine first places in track may remain the high-water mark for many Olympics to come, for America no longer holds a corner on the market. All over the world there is a rising standard of performance and even the smallest countries are developing athletes of Olympic ability.

The United States has helped many small nations under a State Department program by sending coaches and athletes all over the world to teach them techniques in athletics. More and more young men are coming to America as college students and learning these techniques, and this has helped raise the standard of competition throughout the world. This is all to the good of the Olympics and to sports generally, for the broadening of competition means that the Games will be more interesting and exciting than ever before. Next stop, Tokyo, 1964.

CHAPTER **11**

OLYMPIC FACTS AND TALES

THE MEANING OF THE RINGS

The five rings or circles that form the Olympic symbol represent the five major continents of the world. The rings are linked together to denote the sporting friendship of the peoples of the earth, whatever their creed or country. The colors, from left to right, are blue, yellow, black, green, and red, and they were chosen because at least one of them appears in the flag of every nation in the world. The Olympic flag, which was displayed for the first time at the Games in Antwerp in 1920, has a white background with no border, and has the five interlocked rings in the center.

123

NUMBER OF OLYMPIC SPORTS, SUMMER GAMES

Of the 21 sports recognized by the International Olympic Committee at least 15 must be on the program of the Olympic Games. Only sports widely practiced in at least 25 countries, 12 of which must enter, may be included. Below are the recognized sports:

Archery — men and women
Athletics (Track and Field) — men and women
Basketball
Boxing
Canoeing — men and women
Cycling
Equestrian Games — men and women
Fencing — men and women
Field Handball
Field Hockey
Football (soccer)
Gymnastics — men and women
Modern Pentathlon
Rowing
Shooting
Swimming — men and women
Volleyball — men and women
Water Polo
Weight Lifting
Wrestling — free style and Greco-Roman
Yachting — men and women

The following sports listed were those which were on official programs in previous Games but are not now recognized. Last year of competition is shown in parentheses.

Court Tennis (1908)
Football (Rugby) (1932)
Gliding (1936)
LaCrosse (1908)
Motor Boating (1908)
Polo (1936)
Racquets (1908)
Tennis — men and women (1924)

The following sports were listed as demonstrations. The last year held is shown in parentheses:

    Baseball (1956)
    Basque Pelota (1924)
    Football (Australian) (1956)
    Football (USA collegiate) (1932)
    LaCrosse (1948)
    Pesapallo (Finnish baseball) (1952)

WINTER GAMES

The officially recognized winter sports are:

    Biathlon — skiing and shooting
    Bobsledding (not on 1960 program)
    Curling (not on 1960 program)
    Figure Skating — men and women
    Ice Hockey
    Luge — small sled (not on 1960 program)
    Skiing — men and women
    Speed Skating — men and women

The following sports appeared on previous programs either as official or demonstration events:

    *Curling (German) (1936)
    *Dog Sled Racing (1932)
    Ice Dancing — men and women (1948)
    Military Ski Patrol (1948)
    *Skeleton Sled (cresta) (1948)
    Winter Pentathlon (1948)
    *Official events.

MAKING THE TEAM

Since 1896, when the modern Games were revived, a total of some 50,000 athletes from more than 90 nations have competed and almost all of them had to earn their team berths through trials or test matches of one sort or another conducted by their respective countries.

There is no age limit in the Olympics. Sonja Henie was 10 years old when she first skated in the Olympics and Artur von Pongracz was 72 when he made the Austrian equestrian team and competed in

Berlin in 1936. The youngest champion ever crowned was 12-year-old Aileen Riggin who won the springboard diving event for the United States in 1920.

There is no limit to the number of Olympic Games in which an athlete may participate as long as he remains an amateur and makes his country's team. Many athletes have appeared in three Olympic Games and a few in four.[1] Ralph C. Craig won the 100- and 200-meter dashes for the United States at Stockholm in 1912 and 36 years later again made the Olympic team, but this time as a yachtsman, competing in the London Games in 1948.

Olympic athletes come in all sizes and shapes as well as ages. Sonja Henie must have been the smallest, when she competed at the age of 10, for she stood only 5 feet and weighed about 100 pounds when she was fully grown. One of the shortest male champions was America's Joe De Pietro, winner of the bantamweight class in weight lifting in 1948. Joe stood 4 feet 6 inches. On the same team was one of the tallest athletes to perform in the Olympics. He was Bob Kurland of Oklahoma, a 7-foot basketball player.[2] The heaviest? Paul Anderson, a weight lifter from Georgia, tipped the scales at 304 pounds at Melbourne in 1956, but he was topped by Argentina's Humberto Selvetti, who weighed 316 pounds. Both men, incidentally, lifted exactly the same total number of pounds in the heavyweight class final but instead of the result being declared a tie, Anderson was awarded first place because he weighed less than his opponent. This was in accordance with the Olympic weight-lifting rules. That was how the massive 304-pound Anderson won an Olympic championship — for being the lighter man.

The Olympic rules state that each nation is limited to three entries for each individual event. This rule was passed to reduce the number of trial heats that used to clutter up the track and slow down the Games, to say nothing of fatiguing the athletes in the days when there was no limit on the number of entries. Even with the new rule, though, an Olympic team can number as many as 510 athletes, which was the size of Russia's big team in 1956.

On the other hand, there have been several one-man teams. A striking example of this was Chung Cheng-Liu, a sprinter who was

[1] Norman C. Armitage, a fencer, competed for the United States in the 1932, 1936, 1948, 1952, and 1956 Olympic Games.
[2] Tallest of all, perhaps, was Yan Kruminsh, a 7-foot, 3-inch basketball player on the 1960 Russian team.

A child Olympic champion was 13-year-old Marjorie Gestring, winner of the springboard diving event for the United States in 1936 at Berlin.

the sole representative of China's 400,000,000 people at Los Angeles in 1932. (Chung was eliminated in the first 200-meter trial heat.)

Ralph Craig, who switched from track and field to yacht racing, is one of a very few competitors who has changed sports and made his country's team in both. A more recent example is Evgeny Grishin, who was a cyclist on Russia's 1952 Olympic team at Helsinki, but switched to speed skating and became the best in the world, winning championships at Cortina in 1956 and at Squaw Valley four years later.

Had he won a gold medal at cycling, he would have accomplished what only one man has been able to do in Olympic history, which is to win a championship in both the summer and winter Games. The only man who did it is America's Eddie Eagan, light heavyweight boxing champion at Antwerp in 1920, and member of the winning four-man bobsled team at Lake Placid, New York, in 1932.

AMATEURISM

Before an athlete can compete he must sign a statement saying that he is an amateur, which is defined by the Olympic rule as follows: "An amateur is one who participates and always has participated in sport solely for pleasure and for physical, mental, or social benefits he derives therefrom, and to whom participation in sport is nothing more than recreation without material gain of any kind, direct or indirect."

Not eligible for the Olympics are those who have taken money for competing or coaching; those who have decided to become professional athletes and are participating as amateurs to increase their commercial value, and those who have neglected their usual vocation or employment for sport competition.

Much criticism has recently been directed at the Soviet competitors on the grounds that they are "state" athletes supported by the Russian Government, that they are without employment, and do nothing all year but train for the next Games. In line with this, Evgeny Grishin, Russia's cyclist-speed skater, has admitted, "I was in training 12 months a year, six months on bicycle and six months on skates."

At Squaw Valley a *New York Times* reporter questioned several Russian winners as to their occupation, and the response was always "teacher of anatomy" or "student of anatomy."

"Are there any doubts," wrote the *Times* reporter, "about where their tuition and pay checks, not to mention their working schedules, are coming from?"

On the American side as well, "amateurism" is becoming increasingly difficult to define, especially the rule about those who "have neglected their usual vocation or employment for sport competition."

"Is a girl who blandly admits she has taken three years out from a normal course of life 'to be a ski bum' following a 'usual vocation'?" asked the *Times*. "What, then, is the vocation: Skiing?"

"Is a girl skater who talks of having practiced six to eight hours a day for 10 years an amateur?" asked the *Times*. "How does the monetary outlay of 25,000 hours of skating-rink time and coaching stack up against the $14 wrist watch that the Olympic amateur rules say you can't accept? This is not to imply that any rules have been broken," continued the *Times*. "It is simply to question whether the rules mean much, in Baron de Coubertin's terms."

HORSES IN THE OLYMPICS

As long ago as 680 B.C. the horse made its appearance in the Olympics, when four-horse chariot racing was introduced in the hippodrome at Olympia, and the first race was won by Pagondas of Thebes.

The chariots were low and open at the back with the wheels equally low, and the four horses were harnessed in an even line. The two central ones alone were attached to the chariot, while the outsiders, fastened only by leather thongs, ran at a gallop and forced themselves into the front of the team. The charioteer held the reins with his two hands, yet managed to keep the whip in one of them. Because there were no heats and therefore, only one race, all the chariots started off together.

In the huge hippodrome, which was over 100 yards wide and about 400 yards long there was room enough for 40 chariots to start at once. There were two turning points in the course, one at each end of the hippodrome, and the chariots had to go around them 12 times. But it is certain that not many of them reached the finish line. Some were overturned, others locked wheels and could not continue, and there were many collisions, crashes, and jams. It was a wild race, one of confusion, din, action, and dust, yet it must have been an exciting and magnificent sight.

There were also two-horse chariot races and some with two mules, and in the year A.D. 67, as noted before, Nero, the Emperor of Rome, drove a 10-horse chariot, a sight witnessed only once at Olympia.

The four-horse chariot races lasted nearly 300 years but besides these races there were also horse races at Olympia. These were introduced in 648 B.C. and went on for many centuries. In these races it was the custom of the riders on approaching the finish to leap down from their horses and run beside them, holding them by the bridles to the end of the race. The prizes and olive wreaths were given to the owners of the horses, never to the rider or driver. In the ancient Olympics the horse was part of the Games until the end.

In the modern Olympics the animal first made its appearance at Paris in 1900, when polo was introduced. The game has had an on-and-off existence in the Olympics. After 1900 it was part of the program in 1908, 1920, 1924, and 1936, since which time there has been no competition. To Great Britain and Argentina go all the polo

Top, The first hurdle on a curve after the staggered start of the 400-meter hurdle race at Los Angeles in 1932. *Center,* Bob Tisdall of Ireland knocks over the final hurdle, thus depriving himself of a world record, though winning the race. Behind him is second place Glenn Hardin of the United States, who was credited with record time, although he did not win. *Below,* A spill by a member of the Hungarian team in the cross-country race of the three-day event, 1932 Olympics.

honors in the Olympics. Great Britain won the first three championships and Argentina the remaining two.

In 1912 equestrian events were introduced at Stockholm and they have been part of the Games ever since. From that time until 1948 the United States was represented by army teams but since the modern military no longer has any horse units, the Army gave up furnishing the teams. In 1950 a civilian group known as United States Equestrian Team, Inc., was formed and since then America's Olympic teams have been selected and trained by this organization.

Currently on the Olympic program are:

1 — dressage (difficult movements which the horse is taught, known as "high school").

2 — jumping, which is officially listed as *Grand Prix des Obstacles*.

3 — the three-day event, which combines dressage, endurance, (a cross-country race), and jumping. Each competition consumes one day and the series is run off on three consecutive days.

Each of the above-listed events is offered in competition for individuals and also teams. There are, therefore, six equestrian events in all.

The sport, by the way, is open to women. In 1952 Marjorie B. Haines of Gwyned Valley, Pennsylvania, became the first woman member of a United States equestrian team when she rode Flying Dutchman in the dressage team event.

As a rule about 20 nations send equestrian teams to the Olympics and a typical team consists of about ten horses, a dozen riders, and four or five attendants.

The United States has not fared very well in this sport and can claim only two gold medals, both of which were won by army officers in the three-day team event, the first in 1932, the second in 1948. Sweden from the start has been outstanding and has consistently dominated every event except the individual jumping with a record of winning more than a third of the first-place prizes since 1912.

NATIONS THAT EXCEL IN CERTAIN SPORTS

Certain nations, regardless of population, have a tendency to dominate some Olympic sports, and it does not seem to matter whether the sport in which they excel originated in that country and is its national pastime or was adopted by it. For example, water polo, which was first played in England in the 1870's, was taken up by Hungary at a much later date, but in the last five Olympics Hungary has had the winning team four times. Another sport in which the Hungarians have been outstanding is in the two saber events in fencing, individual and team. Hungarian teams have won it eight of the ten times it has been in competition and in the individual they have supplied champions in nine of the last ten Olympics.

By the same token, field hockey, which was developed in England and has been played in the Olympics since 1908 by men only, has been the exclusive property of India in the past six Games. The modern pentathlon[3], which was inaugurated in 1912 as an Olympic event, has been won by Sweden every time except in 1936 when it went to Germany. Soccer football, which is the most universal and international of all team games and is played in almost every country under the sun, attracts some 30 crack teams to the Olympics. No nation has ever had a real hold on the sport, though Great Britain has won the most championships — three since the game was intro-

---

[3] The word "pentathlon" and its use in the Olympics lead to confusion. Originally a 5-event track and field competition consisting of the broad jump, javelin throw, 200-meters run, discus throw, and 1,500-meter run, it was introduced in the Games in 1906 and abandoned after 1924. For placing first in any of the five events a competitor got one point, two for second place, three for third, and so on. The athlete with the lowest score was the winner. It was this pentathlon in which Jim Thorpe excelled. The so-called modern pentathlon is not a track and field event and its competitors are army men. It is supposed to reproduce the hazards a military courier might encounter while carrying a message through hostile country. The first event is a 5,000-meter cross-country ride, on horses drawn by lot. (The courier starts his journey on horseback.) Next is fencing with the epee. (The courier fends off his pursuers with his sword.) The third event is pistol shooting at a "bobbing target" at 25 meters. (Again the courier's pursuers overtake him, but this time he shoots his way out.) Fourth is swimming free style for 300 meters. (The courier, now on foot because his horse has given out, comes to a river and swims across it.) The fifth and final event is running for 4,000 meters, which is about two and a half miles. (Here the courier is on the home stretch and uses his legs to deliver the message.) The modern pentathlon takes five days (one event is held each day) and the scoring is on the same low-point basis as was the old pentathlon. The modern event is sometimes called the "military pentathlon" or merely "pentathlon," since the original one has ceased to exist.

duced in 1900. A surprise winner, however, is little Uruguay with a population of less than 3,000,000 which has twice won the championship (1924 and 1928) and has often defeated such giants as Great Britain, Germany, France, and Italy.

There are seven rowing events on the Olympic slate — single sculls, double sculls, pairs and fours with and without coxswains, and the eight-oared shell. Of the seven the United States has had a worse-than-mediocre record in all but the eight-oared shell. In this event America has completely dominated the scene, winning 10 championships out of 13. The United States first won when the race was inaugurated in 1900 and since then has continued to win except for 1908 and 1912, when Great Britain took over, and 1960, the year Germany won. Since 1920, the United States has been represented by championship college crews. The list follows:

Year	Champion	Min.	Sec.
1920	United States (Navy)	6:	2.6
1924	United States (Yale)	6:	33.4
1928	United States (California)	6:	3.2
1932	United States (California)	6:	37.6
1936	United States (Washington) . . .	6:	25.4
1948	United States (California)	5:	56.7
1952	United States (Navy)	6:	25.9
1956	United States (Yale)	6:	35.2
1960	Germany	5:	57.18

THE CREW THAT WOULDN'T GIVE UP

From 1920 until 1956 no United States eight had lost even a heat in Olympic competition, and no crew of any country had ever lost a heat and then gone on to win a gold medal. Both of these things happened in Australia in 1956. It is one of the great come-back stories of the Olympics.

That spring Yale had won the intercollegiate title and had defeated in the Olympic trials the Naval Academy crew that had won for the United States at Helsinki in 1952. Crew experts rated the Yale aggregation as one of the best ever to sit in a shell. It was the overwhelming favorite to win the Olympics.

It is not difficult, then, to imagine the shock Americans got when Yale in the very first heat finished third behind Australia and Canada. All was not yet lost, though. In Olympic rowing there is a system known as *repechage,* where losers in a first-round heat are not eliminated (as they would be in track and swimming) but are given another chance to row in an extra heat. If they should lose there, however, they are finished. The word *repechage* means second chance.

It was a grim American crew, the first ever to go into *repechage,* that lined up against Italy, Great Britain and France a couple of days later for its final chance. The Yale eight took no chances. They got the lead, held it, and won by two lengths. Next day, in the first of two semi-final heats, Yale was pitted against Russia, Japan, and Australia, the crew that had beaten them in the first-round heat. It was an "all-out" effort by the Americans. They fought past the Aussies with a desperate effort in the last 10 strokes to win by a few feet. Russia and Japan were eliminated. The Aussies, however, were gleeful, feeling that the American eight had rowed itself "straight out" and could not recover for the final. "The first two crews qualified anyway, so why exert yourselves unnecessarily?" the Australians asked.

In the other semi-final that day Canada and Sweden finished one-two and eliminated Czechoslovakia and Italy. Next day in the final, the United States, Australia, Canada, and Sweden lined up on the 2,000-meter course (about one and a fourth miles) on Lake Wendouree, near Melbourne. Forty thousand people gathered along the banks of the lake to see if the impossible could happen — if Yale, having lost its first race, could now win three days in a row.

At 300 meters Canada led, at 400 meters Australia took over, then Canada regained the lead, and at 800 meters the Aussies caught them again. Yale was already hitting 36 strokes to the minute, which was one or two above their normal beat. They got up with the leaders at the halfway mark and then, with 600 meters to go, they went up to a fantastic 40 strokes a minute, held it all the way to the finish line, and nosed across with a half-length lead and victory — the eighth straight eight-oared championship for the United States in Olympic rowing.

"This was a real comeback," wrote crew manager Thomas D. Bolles in the I.O.C. official report of the 1956 Games, "and a great finish for the young men from Yale. Sometime it may be equalled but I doubt that it will ever be exceeded."

134

THE MARATHON

Perhaps the most dramatic single event of the Olympics is the marathon, which, although it was never a part of the ancient Games at Olympia, originated on Greek soil.

In 490 B. C. Miltiades, a Greek general commanding a force of 10,000 warriors, met the invading Persians on the plain of Marathon, which is along the seacoast in Attica, some 25 miles northeast of Athens. Although the Persians outnumbered the Greeks 10 to 1, they were routed by the fury of the Greek phalanx attack, a formation like a flying wedge in football, and were chased back into the sea.

Meanwhile in Athens the elders gravely gathered in the public square to await the news from Marathon. A Greek defeat would mean the downfall of Athens.

When the Persians fled to their ships, Miltiades called for Pheidippides, a famous long distance runner, and told him to carry the good news to the people of Athens. Although Pheidippides had fought hard in the battle of Marathon as a common soldier, he cast aside his armor and started off for Athens. The road led across rough country and up and down steep hills, but Pheidippides kept on going and never stopped. Exhausted and with his feet bleeding, he staggered into the city and came to the elders.

"Rejoice! We conquer!" he cried, then dropped to the ground and died.

The marathon, which approximates the distance from Athens to the site of the famous battle, commemorates the heroic feat of Pheidippides, soldier and athlete.

The race was the feature of the first modern Games at Athens in 1896. Then, as now, it was the last event on the track and field program, the climax of the Games.

Up to the final day of the revived Olympics things had been going poorly for the Greeks. Although the Greek spectators filled the stadium every day and sat on the hills surrounding it, they had not seen a single event won by one of their countrymen. Then came the marathon, over the same course as Pheidippides had taken nearly twenty-four hundred years before. The distance was 40 kilometers, or about 24 miles, 1,500 yards. There were 25 starters in the race and one of them was Spiridon Loues, a little 25-year-old shepherd from Marouissi, who, like Pheidippides, had served in the Greek Army as a common soldier.

At two o'clock on April 10, 1896, a Greek Army officer gave the signal and the 25 runners left the historic plain at Marathon and started on the long, tough road to Athens. All along the way the road was lined with Greek peasants who hoped to see one of their countrymen in the lead, but for the first half of the distance they saw instead the Frenchman, Lermusiaux, who was followed by Flack, the Australian, and Blake, the American.

At the village of Pikermi, Loues, who had spent the previous night praying for victory, asked the peasants how many were ahead of him. Upon being told, he replied, "Do not fear, I will overtake them."

At the next village, 23 kilometers from Marathon, the Frenchman still led, but Blake dropped out from exhaustion. After 32 kilometers the Frenchman collapsed and at the village of Ampelokipi the little Greek shepherd caught up with Flack, who was tiring badly, and took over the lead. The countryside went wild with joy. Mounted messengers galloped ahead to the stadium to tell the king the good news. Quickly the word spread about the crowd, and all eyes were fixed on the gate. Finally, the little peasant appeared and the whole stadium gave him a tremendous ovation. The king's two sons, Prince Constantine and Prince George, ran out of the royal box and trotted about the track with Loues to the finish line. Then they picked him up bodily and carried him to their father. Everyone wanted to thrust presents upon Loues. A lady tore a gold watch from her dress and gave it to him. A bootblack promised to shine his shoes free for life. A barber said that he would cut his hair and shave him without charge as long as he lived. A clothier offered to clothe him on the same terms, and a restaurant owner said that he'd give him free meals forever.

More joy was in store for the happy crowd. The second and third runners to cross the finish line were Greeks, too. Although they had been without victory all through the Games, the Greeks made a clean sweep of the marathon. Loues ran the distance in 2 hours, 55 minutes, and 20 seconds.

The long, grueling race, now standardized throughout the world at 26 miles, 385 yards, is run today in about two hours and a half, which breaks down to just under six minutes per mile. This is remarkable time, when it is considered that the marathoner has to maintain

1896 (Athens)- **SPIRIDON LOUES,** a shepherd, gains glory for Greece in the traditional marathon at the first modern Olympic Games. Princes Constantine and George escort him to victory...

1904 (St. Louis)-The Big Hoax. Marathoner **FRED LORZ** hops a ride in a new-fangled horseless carriage, almost gets the prize.

1908 (London)-Marathon Muddle. While officials drag Italy's Dorando over the finish line, winner **JOHNNY HAYES** (USA) is ignored....

this speed for 26 miles over an up-and-down rough course, never on a level track. The average Olympic field today numbers about 65, of which 15 or 20 men drop out along the way. Plain exhaustion is the chief reason for the collapse of a marathon runner, and many of them have been carried from the roadside right to the hospital. A few have died. Stomach and leg cramps are another reason that some runners are forced to give up, and sometimes cut and bleeding feet are a cause. When Joie Ray, America's hope in the 1928 Olympics at Amsterdam, came home his feet were so raw and swollen that his shoes had to be cut off.

Strange and sometimes funny things have happened in the Olympic marathon. In 1900 the runners covered a 25-mile course through the Bois de Boulogne and a maze of Parisian streets. There was much confusion among the officials in trying to check the runners and keep them from going astray. At Athens the road was patrolled by mounted policemen and lined with spectators. There was nothing like that at Paris and there is no doubt that some of the runners got off the course, accidentally or otherwise. In any event, when the American favorite, Arthur Newton, took the lead at midway and was never passed on the road, he fully expected to be hailed as the winner when he trotted into the arena — but lo! he discovered that the race was all over. Three Frenchmen and a Swede had finished before him. Michel Teato, a French baker boy, is officially credited with the victory, but how he could have won still remains a mystery. He never passed the leader, Arthur Newton, and was never in front of him. The Frenchman got the gold medal but Olympic historians have often referred to Teato as a "highly dubious victor."

In the 1904 Games at St. Louis one of the American starters in the marathon was Fred Lorz of the Mohawk Athletic Club. Fred was going along with the leaders and looked like a possible winner, when he was suddenly seized with cramps a few miles from the stadium and had to quit. Accompanying the runners were four or five chugging autos of 1904 vintage. Fred hailed one and hitched a ride. It was no secret. Several runners saw him board the car and he waved to them as he passed by. Five miles from the stadium the auto broke down and Fred, now fully recovered, hopped out and breezed along on foot. Later, he said he did this to keep from stiffening up and catching cold. Meanwhile, the crowd in the stadium, having been posted on the progress of the race, expected to see the leader, T. J. Hicks of the United States, come through the gate at any moment. Instead, they saw Fred, alone and smiling. Thousands rose to their feet and cheered him as the winner while he circled the track and crossed the finish line. Thoroughly enjoying the glorious joke, Fred took a deep bow before Alice Roosevelt, the President's daughter, who was distributing the prizes in the name of the United States. She was just about to crown him with an olive wreath and hand him a gold medal when someone discovered that Fred was an impostor and started to yell. The hoax was uncovered. Later, Fred said that he had no intention of continuing the joke, but that he could not resist the cheers of the crowd. Nevertheless, the A.A.U. banned him for life, then at a later date reinstated him.

In 1908 the marathon started at Windsor Castle so that the royal British children could see the start. From there to the Olympic Stadium in London the distance was 26 miles with an added 385 yards for the final run on the cinder track for part of a lap to the finish below the royal box. This distance (42.263 kilometers) is now the official one for all marathons, and it is not the exact length of Pheidippides' heroic run though many people think it is. It is 26 miles, 385 yards, because the British princelings wanted to see the start, one of whom, incidentally, is the present Duke of Windsor.

At a signal from Her Royal Highness, the Princess of Wales, Lord Desborough fired the starting gun and the field got off. Among the 58 runners were Dorando Pietri, a little Italian candy maker, Johnny Hayes, a 20-year-old American from New York, and the favorite, C. Hefferon of South Africa.

Eighty thousand people were in the huge stadium at London waiting excitedly for the first runner to come through the gate, when Dorando staggered into view. A great roar greeted him but the sound quickly died down when the crowd saw him glance dazedly around, start in the wrong direction, and then fall on his face. Some British officials, who had done almost everything to ruin the 1908 Games all week long, reached down and grabbed the half-conscious runner, lifted him to his feet, and then, believe it or not, with one on each side of him, dragged him across the finish line. Anything to beat an American, who at that moment was Johnny Hayes, the second runner to enter the gate. Johnny, as fresh as a starting sprinter, turned

in the proper direction, circled the track, and crossed the line. Meantime, the Italian flag had been hoisted and the British officials were hailing Dorando as the victor. Of course, he was not, for he did not finish under his own power. Being picked up and carried as he was meant automatic disqualification. Not until a protest was lodged by the United States, however, was the Italian flag run down and Johnny Hayes declared the winner. For two and a half hours Dorando lay between life and death, but he recovered and was consoled by receiving a special gold trophy, awarded by Queen Alexandra the next day. Later Hayes and Dorando turned professional and started a marathon craze in America. They ran against each other twice in 1909 in Madison Square Garden for a share of the gate receipts. Dorando won both races and in a third match, held outdoors at the Polo Grounds, 30,000 people were on hand to see the marathoners run around and around the ball park for a prize of $10,000. In this race a Frenchman named St. Ives beat both Dorando and Hayes. Incidentally, John J. Hayes, is today a New York food broker of 70-odd years and since he won in London in 1908 the United States has never produced another Olympic marathon winner.

140

Left, A typical marathon start, in which the field gets off casually in an easy trot. *Right,* Olympic judges at the finish line of a sprint.

A damper was cast on the marathon of 1912 at Stockholm when the Portuguese runner, Lazaro, literally ran himself to death. He collapsed at the nineteenth mile and was taken to a hospital, where he expired. Because of his death the marathoners at Antwerp in 1920 were subjected to strict physical examinations. The 1920 race was won, as mentioned before on these pages, by the great Hannes Kolehmainen, the first of the so-called Flying Finns.

In 1924 the marathon was won by A. O. Stenroos, another Flying Finn, with America's entry, Clarence De Mar, taking third place. The international flavor of the marathon is shown in the following list of winners in subsequent Olympics: An Arab named El Ouafi, representing France, won it in 1928; an Argentinian, Zabala, was the victor in 1932; and a Japanese, K. Son, came home first at Berlin in 1936. The crown went back to Argentina in 1948 when Delfo Cabrera won it in a thrilling finish on the track in the London Stadium as he passed Belgian's Etienne Gailly a few yards from the tape. Gailly, who was the first man to enter the stadium, was in pitiful shape and at the finish he collapsed in a heap. He was placed on a stretcher and carried to the arena turf, where he lay motionless for 10 minutes. At last he sat up. The victory ceremony was held up almost an hour in the hope that he would be able to take part, but he was unable to do so.

Zatopek, the great Czech, won the race in 1952 at Helsinki in brilliant time, as noted before, and four years later at Melbourne finished sixth, at last defeated by his old rival, Alain Mimoun, the French Algerian.

The start of the marathon at Melbourne deserves mention here. In any long-distance race the start is not considered important. Generally the runners stand casually about near the starting point. The crouching start is never used, and when the gun goes off they all break into an easy trot. Of course, the start in a sprint or any of the shorter races is very important and may mean victory or defeat. But in a long-distance race it doesn't matter whether the runners get off together or not.

At Melbourne 46 marathon runners stood about in 80-degree heat chatting with one another and waited for the official to start the race. Finally he eyed the men and said, "On your marks. Get set," and fired the starting gun. Unhurriedly the men trotted forward and the race was on — but wait! Twice more in rapid succession the gun barked — the traditional signal of a false start. It commands the runners to stop and return to the mark. Although the runners had 26 miles and 385 yards to go, one of them had beaten the gun and thus had an unfair advantage over the others. So thought the starter, at any rate, so he called them all back and started them over again. Undoubtedly this was the first and only false start in the history of the marathon. Yes, strange things do happen in the marathon.

SPORTSMANSHIP

In the history of the modern Olympics there have been remarkably few disagreeable incidents and examples of poor sportsmanship. In some of the rough contact sports, such as water polo, soccer football, and ice hockey, where the action is fast and young men slam into each other, there have been a few brawls. But the wonder is that there have not been more when you think of the great number of highly spirited athletes from all corners of the earth who are thrown together in the fierceness of competition. I think it is safe to say that in any one Olympics — a period of 16 days — there are fewer fouls committed and fewer penalties imposed than one sees in the average college football game.

The Olympic athlete is fully aware that his country is judged by his conduct on the field and for this reason the Games stand above all other athletic contests in true sportsmanship, in the universal desire to play fair.

Most of the unpleasant incidents have been because of the blundering of officials rather than the bad behavior of the athletes. There have been mix-ups galore but the athlete cannot be faulted because of them.

A classic mix-up occurred in the 1948 winter Games when America sent two hockey teams to St. Moritz, one backed by the Amateur Hockey Association and the other by the Amateur Athletic Union. Which one represented the United States? The Swiss host committee said that the A.H.A. team did, whereupon the United States threatened to withdraw entirely from the winter Games. The mess was put before the I.O.C. for a ruling the day before the Games were scheduled to start. The I.O.C. banned both American teams and declared hockey a "non-Olympic" event. The Swiss ignored the ban and let the A.H.A. team play. Whenever they played, the other American team sat in the stands and booed. Then the I.O.C. met again, reinstated hockey as an official Olympic event, and declared the A.H.A. team null and void. With such a mess it is not surprising that neither American team got anywhere in the tournament.

There have been other mix-ups such as the one in Los Angeles in 1932 when the official who was holding up the lap numbers for the runners in the 3,000-meter steeplechase got confused and held up the wrong number. An extra lap was run. Whether that made any difference in the result of the race will never be known.

For every mix-up and unpleasantness there have been many more examples of sportsmanship. Taking the same 1932 Games as an example of a typical Olympics, this is what we find in the line of sportsmanship:

There were two defending champions in the 400-meter hurdles, Lord David Burghley of Great Britain, the 1928 winner, and Morgan Taylor of the United States, who had won in 1924. The men had met many times on the track. At Los Angeles Lord Burghley decided to stay out of the leg-tiring opening day ceremony parade to save himself for his hurdle race the next day. But when he heard that his rival, Morgan Taylor, had been chosen to carry the American flag and would therefore have to parade, the Englishman insisted on taking part in the parade himself. The sporting gesture was appreciated but the race was won by Bob Tisdall of Ireland, who also marched in the parade. Taylor ran third and Lord Burghley fourth.

In those Games there was a tiny Japanese who was hopelessly outclassed in the 10,000-meter run but he was determined to finish, even though he had been lapped at least once by most of the field. The little plodder realized that he was in the way and forcing swifter runners to run outside of him when they passed him. He reasoned that the leaders — Janusz Kusocinski of Poland and the Flying Finns, Iso-Hollo and Virtanen — might have a better chance to break the record if they didn't have to run around him, so he ran the last several laps out in the third lane. The runners then passed him on the inside, saving time and distance, and the winner, Kusocinski, broke an Olympic record that stood for 16 years. The little Japanese finished all by himself, a lonely last, but he was rewarded with tremendous applause from the admiring crowd.

Again in the 1932 Games there was another example of good sportsmanship, although it didn't look like that in the beginning. It happened in the 5,000 meters at the end of the race when the runners were coming down the stretch and it was a duel between Lauri Lehtinen, a Finn, and Ralph Hill of Oregon. The Finn was leading but at his heels was Ralph Hill, a step behind. As the two swung into the final straightaway, the crowd went wild at the sight of the stirring battle. Down toward the tape they came, and Hill in a supreme effort went to the outside to pass Lehtinen, who was on the pole. Just as he did, the Finn swung out, too, and blocked his way. Hill had to break his stride and pull up. Then Hill switched and tried to pass the Finn on the inside but Lehtinen swerved in and again blocked the American. Finally they crossed the finish line so close that it looked like a dead heat, but the films showed that the Finn had won. The crowd, having seen how Hill had been blocked, began to boo the announcement of the victory — until a few words over the loud-speaker quieted them. "Remember, please, these people are our guests," said the announcer, and the boos turned to applause.

Lehtinen was not aware that he had interfered with Hill on the homestretch. He swerved out and then in, not to block Hill but because he was simply done in with exhaustion. There was no formal protest after the race. When Lehtinen saw the films of the finish he felt so badly about it that at first he did not want to accept the gold medal. He was most upset and apologized to Hill. Later, when he stood on the top step reserved for the winner, he reached down and put his arm around Hill on the step below and tried to draw him up even with him. Hill had the good grace to refuse. The two men became friends, thus happily ending an unfortunate incident in the name of good sportsmanship.

1932 (Los Angeles)—
LAURI LEHTINEN (Finland)
provokes rhubarb by
blocking out RALPH
HILL (USA) to
win 5,000
meters...

THE SWIMMERS

As old as track and field in the modern Olympics is the sport of swimming which was included in the 1896 Games at Athens and has been part of every Olympics since then. Some of the earlier events would bring smiles to the modern Olympic swimmers. There was, for instance, a contest called "100 meters free style between sailors" and another for underwater swimmers for distance. There was also the plunge for distance and other events long since obsolete.

In 1912, at Stockholm, the sport had evolved into something like its present status and women were allowed to compete for the first time. It was in those Games that America produced its first great swimmer in the person of Duke Kahanamoku of Hawaii.

The Duke contributed the "flutter kick" to swimming and was the first man to swim 100 yards in less than a minute. He used his famous crawl stroke to lower the time to 53 seconds. The six-foot-one-inch Hawaiian competed in four Olympic Games over an amazing range of years. He won the 100 meters at Stockholm in 1912 and eight years later (World War I caused abandonment of the 1916 Games) again set the swiftest pace, at Antwerp in 1920. His reign ended in the 1924 Olympics in Paris when the 33-year-old Duke finished a close second to a tall young fellow, Johnny Weissmuller. Illness kept the Duke out of the 1928 Games but in 1932 he tried a comeback. He failed to make the United States Olympic swimming team— after all, he was 41 years old — but he was there in Los Angeles as a member of his country's water polo squad.

Duke Kahanamoku of Hawaii (*left*) competed in four Olympics for the United States and was the country's first great swimming champion. Johnny Weissmuller (*right*) succeeded the Duke as America's swimming champion of the 1920's. He in turn was succeeded by Buster Crabbe, Olympic champion in 1932. Both champions later became "Tarzans" in the movies.

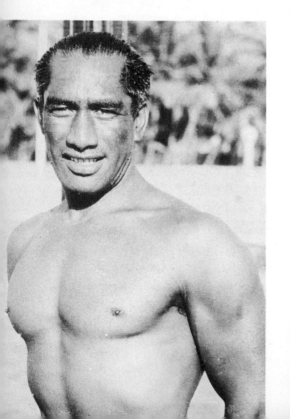

Mrs. Pat McCormick of Long Beach, California, won two diving championships (springboard and platform) in the 1952 Olympics, then did it again
at Melbourne four years later. She is the only diver to score a double-
double.

The great Johnny Weissmuller broke most of the Duke's records
and wore his mantle for many years. He was perhaps our greatest
swimmer. During his long career he held 67 records, some 50 of
which were of major importance and remained on the books for
nearly two decades. He set world records in winning the 100- and
400-meter freestyle events in the 1924 Games at Paris, and in the
1928 Games at Amsterdam he again won the 100-meter championship and was anchorman on the winning 800-meter relay team.

In 1950, when an Associated Press poll named him "the greatest swimmer of the past 50 years," many a teenager read the news
with surprise. They knew Johnny Weissmuller as a tree-climbing
hero of the movie jungles — as Tarzan — and had no idea that he
was once the outstanding swimmer of his day.

Oddly, the Olympics produced another champion swimmer who
became a Tarzan in the movies. Clarence (Buster) Crabbe won the
400-meter free-style for the United States at Los Angeles in 1932
and then, like Weissmuller, turned his talents to vine-swinging for
the film makers.

The Berlin swimming stadium, 1936 Games, seated 18,000 people and it was filled every day.

The 1932 Games, by the way, marked the rise of Japan as a swimming power and the eclipse of the United States. In the six swimming races for men, the Japanese won five, Buster Crabbe's victory being the only one that went to America. In the women's events it was a different matter, however, thanks to the great Helene Madison who won the 100- and 400-meter freestyle races and swam anchor on the victorious 400-meter relay team.

Japanese domination continued until after World War II, when the United States again forged to the front, beginning with the London Games in 1948. It was a dramatic turnabout. America swept the pool and won every title. One of the American champions was Jimmy McLane, a 17-year-old Andover schoolboy who won the 1,500-meter freestyle and, as a member of the winning 800-meter relay team, helped set a world record in that race.

The United States held its own in 1952 (although not in the women's events) but four years later, at Melbourne, the Australians took over and swept the pool almost as impressively as the United States had in 1948. The Aussies won five of the seven men's swimming races and the only American victory was in the 200-meter butterfly stroke, a new event, which was won by William Yorzyk.

All through the ups and downs the United States has known in Olympic swimming the country has been most consistent in turning out diving champions, both men and women, in the springboard (or fancy) diving and the high (or platform) diving. Since 14-year-old Aileen Riggin first won the springboard diving for the United States in 1920, every championship in that event went to an American girl until 1960, when Germany's Ingrid Kramer won it and also took the platform dive.

Of all the American women diving champions, by far the greatest is Mrs. Patricia McCormick of Long Beach, California. At Helsinki in 1952 the graceful Pat took both diving events, and four years later, at Melbourne, did the same thing again. This unparalleled double-double has not yet been matched.

OLYMPIC RECORDS

1896—ATHENS
1900—PARIS
1904—ST. LOUIS
1906—ATHENS
1908—LONDON
1912—STOCKHOLM
1920—ANTWERP
1924—PARIS
1928—AMSTERDAM
1932—LOS ANGELES
1936—BERLIN
1948—LONDON
1952—HELSINKI
1960—ROME

TRACK AND FIELD — MEN
(Obsolete events not included)

100-Meter Dash

		Sec.
1896	T. E. Burke, U.S.	12
1900	F. W. Jarvis, U.S.	10.8
1904	Archie Hahn, U.S.	11
1906	Archie Hahn, U.S.	11.2
1908	R. E. Walker, South Africa	10.8
1912	R. C. Craig, U.S.	10.8
1920	C. W. Paddock, U.S.	10.8
1924	H. M. Abrahams, Gt. Britain	10.6
1928	Percy Williams, Canada	10.8
1932	Eddie Tolan, U.S.	10.3
1936	Jesse Owens, U.S.	10.3
1948	Harrison Dillard, U.S.	10.3
1952	Lindy J. Remigino, U. S.	10.4
1956	Bobby J. Morrow, U.S.	10.5
1960	Armin Hary, Germany	10.2

200-Meter Dash

		Sec.
1900	J. W. B. Tewksbury, U.S.	22.2
1904	Archie Hahn, U.S.	21.6
1908	R. Kerr, Canada	22.6
1912	R. C. Craig, U.S.	21.7
1920	Allan Woodring, U.S.	22
1924	J. V. Scholz, U.S.	21.6
1928	Percy Wililams, Canada	21.8
1932	Eddie Tolan, U.S.	21.2
1936	Jesse Owens, U.S.	20.7
1948	Mel Patton, U. S.	21.1
1952	Andrew W. Stanfield, U.S.	20.7
1956	Bobby J. Morrow, U.S.	20.6
1960	Livio Berutti, Italy	20.5

400-Meter Run

		Sec.
1896	T. E. Burke, U.S.	54.2
1900	M. W. Long, U.S.	49.4
1904	H. L. Hillman, U.S.	49.2
1906	Paul Pilgrim, U.S.	53.2
1908	W. Halswelle, Gt. Britain (walkover)	50
1912	C. D. Reidpath, U.S.	48.2
1920	B.G.D. Rudd, South Africa	49.6
1924	E. H. Liddell, Gt. Britain	47.6
1928	Ray Barbuti, U.S.	7.8
1932	William Carr, U.S.	46.2
1936	Archie Wiliams, U.S.	46.5
1948	Arthur Wint, Jamaica	46.2
1952	G. Rhoden, Jamaica	45.9
1956	Charles L. Jenkins, U. S.	46.7
1960	Otis Davis, U.S.	44.9

800-Meter Run

		Min.-Sec.
1896	E. H. Flack, Gt. Britain	2:11
1900	A. E. Tysoe, Gt. Britain	2: 1.4
1904	J. D. Lightbody, U.S.	1:56
1906	Paul Pilgrim, U.S.	2: 1.2
1908	M. W. Sheppard, U.S.	1:52.8
1912	J. T. Meredith, U.S.	1:51.9
1920	A. G. Hill, Gt. Britain	1:53.4
1924	D.G.A. Lowe, Gt. Britain	1:52.4
1928	D.G.A. Lowe, Gt. Britain	1:51.8
1932	Thos. Hampson, Gt. Britain	1:49.8
1936	John Woodruff, U.S.	1:52.9
1948	Mal Whitfield, U.S.	1:49.2

1952	Mal Whitfield, U.S. 1:49.2		1952	Emil Zatopek, Czecho... 2:23:03.2
1956	Thomas W. Courtney, U.S. 1:47.7		1956	Alain Mimoun, France.. 2:25
1960	Peter Snell, New Zealand .. 1:46.3		1960	Abebe Bikili, Ethiopia .. 2:15:15.2

1,500-Meter Run
Min.-Sec.

1896 E. H. Flack, Gt. Britain...... 4:33.2
1900 C. Bennett, Gt. Britain....... 4: 6
1904 J. D. Lightbody, U.S. 4: 5.4
1906 J. D. Lightbody, U.S. 4:12
1908 M. W. Sheppard, U.S. 4: 3.4
1912 A.N.S. Jackson, Gt. Britain 3:56.8
1920 A. G. Hill, Gt. Britain..... 4: 1.8
1924 Paavo Nurmi, Finland 3:53.6
1928 H. E. Larva, Finland 3:53.2
1932 Luigi Beccali, Italy 3:51.2
1936 J.E. Lovelock, New Zealand 3:47.8
1948 Henry Eriksson, Sweden 3:49.8
1952 J. Barthel, Luxembourg 3:45.2
1956 Ron Delany, Ireland 3:41.2
1960 Herb Elliott, Australia 3:35.6

110-Meter Hurdles
Sec.

1896 T. P. Curtis, U.S. 17.6
1900 A. E. Kraenzlein, U.S. 15.4
1904 F. W. Schule, U.S. 16
1906 R. G. Leavitt, U.S. 16.2
1908 Forrest Smithson, U.S. 15
1912 F. W. Kelley, U.S. 15.1
1920 E. J. Thomson, Canada 14.8
1924 D. C. Kinsey, U.S. 15
1928 S. Atkinson, South Africa..... 14.8
1932 George Saling, U.S. 14.6
1936 Forrest Towns, U.S. 14.2
1948 William Porter, U.S. 13.9
1952 Harrison Dillard, U.S. 13.7
1956 Lee G. Calhoun, U.S. 13.5
1960 Lee G. Calhoun, U.S. 13.8

5,000-Meter Run
Min.-Sec.

1912 H. Kolehmainen, Finland 14:36.6
1920 J. Guillemot, France 14:55.6
1924 Paavo Nurmi, Finland 14:31.2
1928 Willie Ritola, Finland 14:38
1932 Lauri Lehtinen, Finland.... 14:30
1936 Gunnar Hockert, Finland 14:22.2
1948 Gaston Reiff Belgium 14:17.6
1952 E.Zatopek, Czechoslovakia 14:06.6
1956 Vladimir Kuts, U.S.S.R.... 13:39.6
1960 Murray Halberg, N.Z. 13:43.4

400-Meter Hurdles
Sec.

1900 J. W. B. Tewksbury, U.S. 57.6
1904 H. L. Hillman, U.S. 53
1908 C. J. Bacon, U.S. 55
1920 F. F. Loomis, U.S. 54
1924 F. Morgan Taylor, U.S. 52.6
1928 Lord Burghley, Gt. Britain.... 53.4
1932 Robert Tisdall, Ireland 51.8
1936 Glenen Hardin, U.S. 52.4
1948 Roy Cochran, U.S. 51.1
1952 Charles Moore, U.S. 50.8
1956 Glenn A. Davis, U.S. 50.1
1960 Glenn A. Davis, U.S. 49.3

10,000-Meter Run
Min.-Sec.

1912 H. Kolehmainen, Finland 31:20.8
1920 Paavo Nurmi, Finland 31:45.8
1924 Willie Ritola, Finland 30:23.2
1928 Paavo Nurmi, Finland 30:18.8
1932 Janusz Kusocinski, Poland 30:11.4
1936 Ilmari Salminen, Finland 30:15.4
1948 E.Zatopek, Czechoslovakia 29:59.6
1952 E.Zatopek, Czechoslovakia 29:17.0
1956 Vladimir Kuts, U.S.S.R.... 28:45.6
1960 P. Bolotnikov, U.S.S.R. 28:32.2

3,000-Meter Steeplechase
Min.-Sec.

1920 P. Hodge, Gt. Britain 10: 4
1924 Willie Ritola, Finland 9:33.6
1928 T. A. Loukola, Finland.... 9:21.8
1932 V. Iso-Hollo, Finland 10:33.4
    (3,460 meters—extra lap by error)
1936 V. Iso-Hollo, Finland 9: 3.8
1948 T. Sjostrand, Sweden 9: 4.6
1952 Horace Ashenfelter, U.S. 8:45.4
1956 Chris Brasher, Gt. Britain 8:41.2
1960 Z. Krzyskowiak, Poland 8:34.2

Marathon
Hr.-Min.-Sec.

1896 S. Loues, Greece 2:55:20
1900 Teato, France 2:59
1904 T. J. Hicks, U.S. 3:28:53
1906 W. Sherring, Canada 2:51:23.6
1908 John J. Hayes, U.S. 2:55:18.4
1912 K.MacArthur, So. Africa 2:36:54.8
1920 H.Kolehmainen, Finland 2:32:35.8
1924 A. O. Stenroos, Finland 2:41:22.6
1928 El Ouafi, France 2:32:57
1932 Juan Zabala, Argentina 2:31:36
1936 Kitei Son, Japan 2:29:19.2
1948 D. Cabrera, Argentina.... 2:34:51.6

20,000-Meter Walk
Hr.-Min.-Sec.

1956 L. Spirine, U.S.S.R. 1:31.27
1960 V. Golubnichi, U.S.S.R. 1:34:07.2

50,000-Meter Walk
Hr.-Min.-Sec.

1932 T.W. Green, Gt. Britain 4:50:10
1936 H. Whitlock, Gt. Britain 4:30:41.4
1948 J. A. Ljunggren, Sweden 4:41:52

151

1952 G. Dordoni, Italy 4:28:07.8
1956 Norm. Read, N. Zealand 4:30:42.8
1960 D. Thompson, Gt. Brit. 4:25:30

400-Meter Relay

	Sec.
1912 Gt. Brit. (Jacobs, Macintosh, d'Arcy, Applegarth)	42.4
1920 U. S. A. (Charles Paddock, Jackson Scholz, Morris Kirksey, Loren Murchison)	42.2
1924 U.S.A. (Louis Clarke, Francis Hussey, Loren Murchison, Alfred Leconey)	41
1928 U.S.A. (Frank Wycoff, James Quinn, Charles Borah, Henry Russell)	41
1932 U.S.A. (Robert Kiesel, Emmett Toppino, Hector Dyer, Frank Wycoff)	40
1936 U.S.A. (Jesse Owens, Ralph Metcalfe, Foy Draper, Frank Wycoff)	39.8
1948 U.S.A. (Norwood Ewell, Lorenzo Wright, Harrison Dillard, Mel Patton)	40.3
1952 U.S.A. (F. Smith, H. Dillard, L. Remigino, A. Stanfield)	40.1
1956 U.S.A. (I. J. Murchison, L. King, W. T. Baker, B. J. Morrow)	39.5
1960 Germany (B. Cullmann, A. Hary, W. Mahlendorf, M. Lauer)	39.5

1,600-Meter Relay

	Min.-Sec.
1908 U.S.A. (W. F. Hamilton, N. J. Cartmell, B. Taylor, M. W. Sheppard) (200-200-400-800 meters)	3:29.4
1912 U.S.A. (M. W. Sheppard, E. F. Lindberg, J. T. Meredith, C. D. Reidpath)	3:16.6
1920 Gt. Britain (Lindsay, Butler, Ainsworth, Griffiths)	3:22.2
1924 U.S.A. (C. S. Cochran, W. E. Stevenson, J. O. McDonald, Allen Helffrich)	3:16
1928 U.S.A. (George Baird, Fred Alderman, Emerson Spencer, Ray Barbuti)	3:14.2
1932 U.S.A. (Ivan Fuqua, Edgar Ablowich, Karl Warner, William Carr)	3:08.2
1936 Gt. Brit. (Wolff, Rampling, Roberts, Brown)	3:09
1948 U.S.A. (Cliff Bourland, Art Harnden, Roy Cochran, Mal Whitfield)	3:10.4
1952 Jamaica (H. McKenley, L. Laing, A. Wint, G. Rhoden)	3:03.9
1956 U.S.A. (C. L. Jenkins, L. Jones, J. Mashburn, T. J. Courtney)	3:04.8
1960 U.S.A. (J. Yerman, E. Young, G. Davis, O. Davis)	3:02.2

Pole Vault

1896	W. W. Hoyt, U.S.	10′ 9¾″
1900	I. K. Baxter, U.S.	10′ 9.9″
1904	C. E. Dvorak, U.S.	11′ 6″
1906	Gouder, France	11′ 6″
1908	A. C. Gilbert, U.S. E. H. Cook, Jr., U.S.	12′ 2″
1912	H. S. Bakcock, U.S.	12′ 11½″
1920	Frank K. Foss, U.S.	13′ 5″
1924	L. S. Barnes, U.S.	12′ 11½″
1928	Sabin W. Carr, U.S.	13′ 9⅜″
1932	William Miller, U.S.	14′ 1⅞″
1936	Earle Meadows, U.S.	14′ 3¼″
1948	O. Guinn Smith, U.S.	14′ 1¼″
1952	Robert Richards, U.S.	14′ 11¼″
1956	Robert Richards, U.S.	14′ 11½″
1960	Don Bragg, U.S.	15′ 5⅛″

High Jump

1896	E. H. Clark, U.S.	5′ 11¼″
1900	I. K. Baxter, U.S.	6′ 2⅘″
1904	S. S. Jones, U.S.	5′ 11″
1906	Con Leahy, Ireland	5′ 9⅞″
1908	H. F. Porter, U.S.	6′ 3″
1912	A. W. Richards, U.S.	6′ 4″
1920	R. W. Landon, U.S.	6′ 4¼″
1924	H. M. Osborn, U.S.	6′ 5 15/16″
1928	Robert W. King, U.S.	6′ 4⅜″
1932	D. McNaughton, Canada	6′ 5⅝″
1936	C. Johnson, U.S.	6′ 7 15/16″
1948	J. A. Winter, Australia	6′ 6″
1952	W. Davis, U.S.	6′ 8¼″
1956	Charles E. Dumas, U.S.	6′ 11¼″
1960	R. Shavlakadze, U.S.S.R.	7′ 1″

Broad Jump

1896	E. H. Clark, U. S.	20′ 9¾″
1900	A. C. Kraenzlein, U. S.	23′ 6⅞″
1904	Myer Prinstein, U.S.	24′ 1″
1906	Myer Prinstein, U.S.	23′ 7½″
1908	Frank Irons, U.S.	24′ 6½″
1912	A. L. Gutterson, U.S.	24′ 11¼″
1920	W. Pettersson, Sweden	23′ 5½″
1924	DeH. Hubbard, U.S.	24′ 5⅛″
1928	Edward Hamm, U.S.	25′ 4¾″
1932	Edward Gordon, U.S.	25′ ¾″
1936	Jesse Owens, U.S.	26′ 5 5/16″
1948	Willie Steele, U.S.	25′ 8″
1952	J. C. Biffle, U.S.	24′ 10″
1956	Gregory C. Bell, U.S.	25′ 8¼″
1960	Ralph Boston, U.S.	26′ 7¾″

Hop, Step and Jump

1896	J. B. Connolly, U.S.	45′
1900	Myer Prinstein, U.S.	47′ 4¼″
1904	Myer Prinstein, U.S.	47′
1906	P. O'Connor, Ireland	46′ 2″
1908	T. Ahearne, Gt. Britain	48′ 11¼″
1912	G. Lindblom, Sweden	48′ 5⅛″
1920	V. Tuulos, Finland	47′ 6⅞″
1924	A. Winter, Australia	50′ 11⅛″

1928	Mikio Oda, Japan	49′	10 13/16″
1932	Chuhei Nambu, Japan	51′	7″
1936	Naoto Tajima, Japan	52′	5⅞″
1948	A. Ahman, Sweden	50′	6¼″
1952	A. Ferreira da Silva, Brazil	53′	2½″
1956	A. Ferreira da Silva, Brazil	53′	7½″
1960	Jozef Schmidt, Poland	55′	1¾″

16-Lb. Shot Put

1896	R. S. Garrett, U.S.	36′	2″
1900	R. Sheldon, U.S.	46′	3⅛″
1904	Ralph Rose, U.S.	48′	7″
1906	M. J. Sheridan, U.S.	40′	4⅘″
1908	Ralph Rose, U.S.	46′	7½″
1912	P. J. McDonald, U.S.	50′	4″
1920	V. Porhola, Finland	48′	7⅛″
1924	Clarence Houser, U.S.	49′	2½″
1928	John Kuck, U.S.	52′	11/16″
1932	Leo Sexton, U. S.	52′	6 3/16″
1936	Hans Woellke, Germany	53′	1¾″
1948	W. Thompson, U.S.	56′	2″
1948	W. P. O'Brien, Jr., U.S.	57′	1½″
1956	W. P. O'Brien, Jr., U.S.	60′	11″
1960	Bill Nieder, U.S.	64′	6¾″

Discus Throw

1896	R. S. Garrett, U.S.	95′	7½″
1900	R. Bauer, Hungary	118′	2.9″
1904	M. J. Sheridan, U.S.	128′	10½″
1906	M. Sheridan, U.S.	136′	⅓″
1908	M. J. Sheridan, U.S.	134′	2″
1912	A. Taiple, Finland	148′	3.9″
1920	E. Ninklander, Finland	146′	7″
1924	S. Houser, U. S.	151′	5¼″
1928	C. Houser, U.S.	155′	2¾″
1932	John Anderson, U.S.	162′	4⅞″
1936	K. Carpenter, U.S.	165′	7⅜″
1948	A. Consolini, Italy	173′	2″
1952	E. Iness, U. S.	180′	6½″
1956	Alfred A. Oerter, U.S.	184′	10½″
1960	Alfred A. Oerter, U.S.	194′	2″

16-Lb. Hammer Throw

1900	J. J. Flanagan, U.S.	167′	4″
1904	J. J. Flanagan, U.S.	168′	1″
1908	J. J. Flanagan, U.S.	170′	4¼″
1912	M. J. McGrath, U.S.	177′	7″
1920	P. J. Ryan, U.S.	173′	5⅝″
1924	F. D. Tootell, U.S.	174′	10¼″
1928	P. O'Callaghan, Ireland	168′	7½″
1932	P. O'Callaghan, Ireland	176′	11⅛″
1936	Karl Hein, Germany	185′	4¼″
1948	I. Nemeth, Hungary	183′	11½″
1952	J. Csermak, Hungary	197′	11¾″
1956	H. V. Connolly, U.S.	207′	3½″
1960	V. Rudinkov, U.S.S.R.	220′	1¼″

Javelin Throw

1906	E. Lemming, Sweden	175′	6″
1908	E. Lemming, Sweden	179′	10½″
1912	E. Lemming, Sweden	198′	11¼″
1920	Jonni Myra, Finland	215′	9¾″
1924	Jonni Myra, Finland	206′	6¾″
1928	E. Lundquist, Sweden	218′	6⅛″
1932	M. Jarvinen, Finland	238′	7″
1936	G. Stock, Germany	235′	8 5/16″
1948	K. Rautavaara, Finland	228′	10½″
1952	C. C. Young, U.S.	242′	¾″
1956	E. Danielson, Norway	281′	2¼″
1960	V. Tsibulenko, U.S.S.R.	277′	8⅜″

Decathlon

		Points
1912	H. Wieslander, Sweden	7724.49
1920	H. Lovland, Norway	6804.35
1924	H. M. Osborn, U. S.	7710.77
1928	Paavo Yrjola, Finland	8053.29
1932	James Bausch, U.S.	8462.23
	(Old point system used 1912 to 1932)	
1936	Glenn Morris, U.S.	7900
1948	Robert Mathias, U.S.	7139
1952	Robert Mathias, U.S.	7887
1956	Milton G. Campbell, U.S.	7937
1960	Rafer Johnson, U.S.	8392

TRACK AND FIELD — WOMEN

100-Meter Dash

		Sec.
1928	Elizabeth Robinson, U.S.	12.2
1936	Helen Stephens, U.S.	11.5
1932	S. Walasiewiz, Poland	11.9
1948	F. Blankers-Koen, Netherlands	11.9
1952	M. Jackson, Australia	11.5
1956	Betty Cuthbert, Australia	11.5
1960	Wilma Rudolph, U.S.	11.0

200-Meter Dash

1948	F. Blankers-Koen, Netherlands	24.4
1952	M. Jackson, Australia	23.7
1956	Betty Cuthbert, Australia	23.4
1960	Wilma Rudolph, U.S.	24.0

400-Meter Relay

		Sec.
1928	Canada	48.4
1932	United States	47
1936	United States	46.9
1948	Netherlands	47.5
1952	United States	45.9
1956	Australia	44.5
1960	United States	44.5

80-Meter Hurdles

1932	Mildred Didrikson, U.S.	11.7
1936	Trebisonda Villa, Italy	11.7
1948	F. Blankers-Koen, Netherlands	11.2
1952	S. Strickland de la Hunty, Australia	10.9

1956 S. Strickland de la Hunty,
    Australia 10.7
1960 Irina Press, U.S.S.R. 10.8

800-Meter Run
1928 Linda Radke, Germany 2:16.8
1960 L. Shevkova, U.S.S.R. 2:04.3

High Jump
1928 E. Catherwood, Canada.... 5' 3"
1932 Jean Shiley, U.S. .... 5' 5¼"
1936 Ibolya Csak, Hungary .... 5' 3"
1948 Alice Coachman, U.S. .... 5' 6⅛"
1952 E. Brand, South Africa.... 5' 5¾"
1956 Mildred L. McDaniel, U.S. 5' 9¼"
1960 Ioland Balas, Rumania .... 6' ¾"

Discus Throw
1928 H.Konopacka, Poland 129' 11⅞"
1932 L. Copeland, U.S. ...... 133' 2"
1936 G. Mauermayer, Ger. 156' 3³⁄₁₆"
1948 M.Ostermeyer, France 137' 6½"
1952 N. Romaschkova,
    U.S.S.R. .... 168' 8½"

1956 Olga Fikotova, Czech. 176' 1½"
1960 N. Ponomaryeva,
    U.S.S.R. .... 180' 8¼"

Javelin Throw
1932 M. Didrikson, U.S. .... 143' 4"
1936 T. Fleischer, Germany 148' 2¾"
1948 H. Bauma, Austria .... 149' 6"
1952 D.Zatopekova, Czecho. 165' 7"
1956 I. Janzeme, U.S.S.R. .... 176' 8"
1960 E. Ozolina, U.S.S.R. ....183' 8"

8-Lb. 13-4/5 Ozs. Shot Put
1948 M. Ostermeyer, France 45' 1½"
1952 G. Zybina, U.S.S.R. .... 50' 1½"
1956 T. Tishkyvich, U.S.S.R. 54' 5"
1960 Tamara Press, U.S.S.R. 56' 9⅞"

Broad Jump
1948 O. Gyarmati, Hungary 18' 8¼"
1952 Y. Williams, N. Zealand 20' 5¾"
1956 E. Krzeskinka, Poland .. 20' 10"
1960 V. Krepkina, U.S.S.R. .. 20' 10⅞"

WINTER GAMES

1924—Chamonix, France

1928—St. Moritz, Switzerland

1932—Lake Placid, N.Y., U.S.A.

1936—Garmisch-Partenkirchen, Germany

1948—St. Moritz, Switzerland

1952—Oslo, Norway

1956—Cortina, Italy

1960—Squaw Valley, Cal., U.S.A.

ICE HOCKEY

1920 Canada	1948 Canada
1924 Canada	1952 Canada
1928 Canada	1956 Russia
1932 Canada	1960 U. S.
1936 Great Britain	

SKIING — MEN

Cross-Country
15 Kilometers
Hr.-Min.-Sec.
1956 H. Brenden, Norway......... 49:39
1960 Haakon Brusveen, Norway 51:55.5

30 Kilometers
1956 V. Hakulinen, Finland 1:44:06
1960 S. Jernberg, Sweden...... 1:51:03.9

50 Kilometers
1924 T. Haug, Norway 3:44:32
1928 P. Hedlund, Sweden .. 4:52: 3
1932 Veli Saarinen, Finland
    (48,238-m) 4:28
1936 Elis Viklund, Sweden.... 3:30:11
1948 Nils Karlsson, Sweden . 3:47:48
1952 V. Hakulinen, Finland . 3:33:33
1956 S. Jernberg, Sweden...... 2:50:27
1960 K. Hamalainen, Finland 2:59:06.3

Nordic Combined—18-km. Race and Jumping

Points

1924 Thorlief Haug, Norway.... 453.8
1928 J. Grottumsbraaten, Norway 427.8
1932 J. Grottumsbraaten, Norway 446.2
1936 Oddbjorn Hagen, Norway 430.3
1948 Heikki Hasu, Finland 448.8
1952 S. Slattvik, Norway 451.621
1956 S. Stenersen, Norway 455.0
1960 Georg Thoma, Germany.. 457.952

40-Kilometer Relay

Hr.-Min.-Sec.

1936 Finland 2:41:33
1948 Sweden 2:32: 8
1952 Finland 2:20:16
1956 Russia 2:15:30
1960 Finland 2:18:45.6

Ski Jump

Points

1924 Jacob T. Thams, Norway.... 227.5
1928 Alfred Andersen, Norway.... 230.5
1932 Birger Ruud, Norway 228
1936 Birger Ruud, Norway 232
1948 Petter Hugsted, Norway 228.1
1952 A. Bergman, Norway 226.0
1956 Antti Hyvarinen, Finland ... 227.0
1960 H. Recknagel, Germany 227.2

SPEED SKATING — MEN

500 Meters

Sec.

1924 Charles Jewtraw, U.S. 44
1928 Clas Thunberg, Finland, and Bernt Evensen, Norway...... 43.4
1932 John A. Shea, U.S. 43.4
1936 Ivar Ballangrud, Norway........ 43.4
1948 Finn Helgesen, Norway........ 43.1
1952 Ken Henry, U.S. 43.2
1956 Evgenij Grishin, U.S.S.R. 40.2
1960 Evgenij Grishin, U.S.S.R. ... 40.2

1,500 Meters

Min.-Sec.

1924 Clas Thunberg, Finland 2:20.8
1928 Clas Thunberg, Finland 2:21.1
1932 John Shea, U.S. 2:57.5
1936 Charles Mathisen, Norway 2:19.2
1948 Sverre Farstad, Norway...... 2:17.6
1952 H. Andersen, Norway........ 2:20.4
1956 Evgenij Grishin, U.S.S.R. .. 2:08.6
1960 Evgenij Grishin, U.S.S.R. Roald Aaas, Norway.......... 2:11.5

5,000 Meters

1924 Clas Thunberg, Finland...... 8:39
1928 Ivar Ballangrud, Norway.... 8:50.5
1932 Irving Jaffe, U.S. 9:40.8
1936 Ivar Ballangrud, Norway.... 8:19.6
1948 Reidar Liaklev, Norway..... 8:29.4
1952 H. Andersen, Norway........ 8:10.6
1956 Boris Shilkov, U.S.S.R. 7:48.7
1960 Viktor Kosichkin, U.S.S.R. 7:51.3

10,000 Meters

1924 Julien Skutnabb, Finland.. 18: 4.8
1928 No decision, thawing of ice — Irving Jaffee, U.S., had best time of 18:36.5
1932 Irving Jaffee, U.S. 19:13.6
1936 Ivar Ballangrud, Norway.. 17:24.3
1948 Ake Seyffarth, Sweden..... 17:26.3
1952 H. Andersen, Norway..... 16:45.8
1956 Sigvard Ericsson, Sweden 16:35.9
1960 Knut Johannesen, Norway 15:46.6

Downhill Race

Min.-Sec.

1948 Henri Oreiller, France 2:55.0
1952 Z. Colo, Italy 2:30.8
1956 Anton Sailer, Austria 2:52.2
1960 Jean Vuarnet, France 2:06.0

Giant Slalom

1952 S. Eriksen, Norway 2:25.0
1956 Anton Sailer, Austria 3:00.1
1960 Roger Staub, Switzerland.. 1:48.3

Slalom

1948 Edi Reinalter, Switzerland 2:10.3
1952 O. Schneider, Austria 2: 0.0
1956 Anton Sailer, Austria 1:94.7
1960 E. Hinterseer, Austria 2:08.9

Biathlon

1960 Klas Lestander, Sweden 1:33:21.6

BOBSLED

4-Man Bob

Min.-Sec.

1924 Switzerland (Scherrer) 5:45.54
1928 United States (Fiske) 3:20.5
1932 United States (Fiske) 7:53.68
1936 Switzerland (Musy) 5:19.85
1948 United States (Tyler) 5:20.1
1952 Germany (Ostler) 5:07.84
1956 Switzerland (Kapus) 5:10.44
1960 Not contested.

155

2-Man Bob

1932 United States (Stevens).... 8:14.74
1936 United States (Brown).... 5:29.29
1948 Switzerland (Endrich) 5:29.2
1952 Germany (Ostler) 5:24.54
1956 Italy (Costa) 5:30.14
1960 Not contested.

FIGURE SKATING — MEN

Points
1908 Salchow, Sweden 2,641
1920 G. Grafstrom, Sweden ... 2,838.5
1924 G. Grafstrom, Sweden.... 2,575.25
1928 G. Grafstrom, Sweden.... 2,698.25
1932 K. Schaefer, Austria 2,602
1936 K. Schaefer, Austria...... 2,959
1948 R. T. Button, U.S. 191.177
1952 R. T. Button, U.S. 192.256
1956 Hayes A. Jenkins, U.S.   166.43
1960 David Jenkins, U.S. 1,440.2

SKIING — WOMEN

Downhill Race

Min.-Sec.
1948 Hedi Schlunegger, Switz.... 2:28.3
1952 T. Jochum-Beiser, Finland 1:47.1
1956 Madeleine Berthod, Switz.. 1:40.7
1960 Heidi Biebl, Germany....... 1:37.6

10 km. (8 Miles)

1952 L. Wideman, Finland 41:40.0
1956 Ljubovj Kozyreva,
       U.S.S.R. 38:11
1960 Maria Gusakova, U.S.S.R. 39:46.6

Slalom

1948 Gretchen Fraser, U.S. 1:57.2
1952 A. M. Lawrence, U. S. 2:10.6
1956 Renee Colliard, Switzerland 1:12.3
1960 Anne Heggtveit, Canada.... 1:49.6

Giant Slalom

1952 A. M. Lawrence, U.S. 2:06.8
1956 Ossi Reichert, Germany..... 1:56.5
1960 Yvonne Ruegg, Switzerland 1:39.9

Cross Country
3x5 Km. Relay

1960 Sweden 1:04:21.4

SPEED SKATING — WOMEN

500 Meters

1960 Helga Haase, Germany...... 45.9

1,500 Meters

1960 Lydia Skoblikova, U.S.S.R. 2:25.2

1,000 Meters

1960 Klara Guseva, U.S.S.R. 1:34.1

3,000 Meters

1960 Lydia Skoblikova, U.S.S.R. 5:14.3

FIGURE SKATING — WOMEN

Women

1908 Syers, Great Britain 1,767.50
1920 Julin, Sweden 1,278.90
1924 Mrs. H. Szabo-Planck,
       Austria 2,094.25
1928 Sonja Heine, Norway 2,452.25
1932 Sonja Henie, Norway 2,302.5
1936 Sonja Henie, Norway 2,971.4
1948 B. Ann Scott, Canada..   163.077
1952 J. Altwegg, Gt. Britain   161.756
1956 Tenley E. Albright, U.S.   169.67
1960 Carol Heiss, U.S. 1,490.1

Pairs

1908 Miss Hublér and Burger,
       Germany 78.4
1920 Mr. and Mrs. Jacobsson,
       Finland 80.7
1924 H. Engelmann and A. Ber-
       ger, Austria 74.5
1928 Andree Joly and Pierre
       Brunet, France 78.2
1932 Andree and Pierre Brunet,
       France 76.7
1936 Maxie Herber and Ernst
       Baier, Germany 103.3
1948 Micheline Lannoy and Pi-
       erre Baugniet, Belgium   11.227
1952 R. & P. Falk, Germany.... 11.400
1956 Elizabeth Schwarz and K.
       Oppelt, Austria 11.31
1960 B. Wagner, R. Paul,
       Canada 80.4

INDEX

London Olympics (1948), 63, 64, 67, 69, 73-74, 141, 148
Long, Dallas, 111
Lorz, Fred, 138, 139
Los Angeles Olympics (1932), 50, 51, 55, 141, 143-45, 148
Loues, Spiridon, 135, 136
Loukola, Toivo, 42

McCormick, Patricia, 147, 149
McDaniel, Mildred, 89
McLane, Jimmy, 148
Madison, Helene, 148
Marathon winners, 39, 79-80, 89, 121-22, 135-42
Mathias, Charles M., 63
Mathias, Robert Bruce, 63-68, 75
Melbourne Olympics (1956), 80-81, 84, 85, 88, 133-34, 142, 149
Milo of Croton, 10, 11, 12, 18
Mimoun, Alain, 78, 79, 89, 142
Mondschein, Irving, 65
Moody, Helen Wills, 54
Morrow, Bobby Joe, 81, 82, 83, 84, 85

Nambu, Chuhei, 56
New York Athletic Club, 21
New Zealand, at Olympics, 122
Newton, Arthur, 138
Neider, Bill, 111, 112
Norton, Ray, 111, 113, 114, 120
Norway, at Winter Games, 92, 95, 98, 100, 102, 107
Nurmi, Paavo, 28, 38-44, 60

O'Brien, W. Parry, 85, 86, 111
Olympic Creed, 21
Olympic flag, 123
Olympic Games, *1896*, 19-21, 27, 62, 135-36; *1900*, 22, 27-28, 47, 138; *1904*, 22, 23, 138-39; *1906*, 23-24, 28; *1908*, 24, 29, 47, 139; *1912*, 24-25, 29, 32-33, 34, 37, 38, 47, 141; *1920*, 39, 123, 147; *1924*, 40, 47, 141; *1928*, 42, 43, 141; *1932*, 50, 51, 55, 141, 143-44, 148; *1936*, 58-59, 62, 141; *1948*, 63, 64, 67, 69, 73-74, 141, 148; *1952*, 75, 76, 78, 80, 85, 88, 142, 149; *1956*, 80-81, 84, 85, 88, 89, 133-34, 142; *1960*, 109-22; ancient, 7-16, 45; horses in, 129-31; no official scoring at, 42; records at, 150-56; sports recognized at, 124-25; sportsmanship at, 142-45; swimming events at, 145-49; team eligibility for, 125-27
Olympic Jury of Appeal, 73
Olympic oath, 101
Olympic Stadium, Rome, 109
Owens, Jesse, 28, 35, 55-62, 111

Pancratian, 11, 12, 13
Parade of Nations, at Olympics, 47, 72
Parakevopoulos, 27
Paris Olympics (1900), 22, 27-28, 47, 138
Paris Olympics (1924), 40, 47, 141
Patton, Mel, 69, 70, 73
Pentathlon, 10, 12-13, 32, 33, 39, 132 and *n.*
Pheidippides, 135
Pherenice, 45
Pietri, Dorando, 139, 140
Pietro, De, Joe, 126
Pirie, Gordon, 82, 84
Pisidorus, 45
Pitou, Penny, 102, 103, 104
Poland, at Olympics, 89, 122
Pole vault, 33, 88
Polydamas of Thessaly, 12

Radford, Peter, 113
Ray, Joie, 138
Reichert, Ossi, 97
Reiff, Gaston, 79
Relay, 400-meter, 60, 62, 85, 89
Richards, Robert E., 87, 88
Riggin, Aileen, 126, 149
Riley, Jack, 105
Rings, as Olympic symbol, 123
Ritola, Willie, 40, 42, 43
Ritter, Max, 118
Robbins, W. C., 24
Robertson, Lawson, 58
Robinson. Elizabeth, 47
Roles, Barbara, 107